The Case Against the Democratic State

If it be asked, to what purpose it is to turn our Attention to points merely Speculative and visionary? I answer that Speculative points ought not to be excluded from the Circle of human Knowledge. They tend to enlarge our Conceptions & to strengthen our Faculties. Speculation has a like Effect with regard to our intellectual powers as bodily Exercises have, with regard to the health strength and agility of the Body.

Thomas Reid, *Practical Ethics*

The Case Against the Democratic State

An Essay in Cultural Criticism

Gordon Graham

ia

IMPRINT ACADEMIC

Published in the UK by Imprint Academic
PO Box 1, Thorverton EX5 5YX, UK

Published in the USA by Imprint Academic
Philosophy Documentation Center
PO Box 7147, Charlottesville, VA 22906-7147, USA

ISBN 0 907845 38 X

A CIP catalogue record for this book is available from the
British Library and US Library of Congress

Contents

Introduction

The history of the last two hundred years, at least in Europe, is a story of the immense and relentless growth of one social institution at the expense of others. I mean the State. Whereas at one time, the State was an institution whose power and importance could be challenged and checked — chiefly, though not exclusively, by the Christian church — it has emerged into the present day as the dominant social institution, and dominant to an enormous degree. It is the case for instance, that in almost every developed country the State is the largest employer, the largest investor, the principal educator, the main provider of health services and social security, the regulator of families, voluntary organizations and companies, and the administrator of justice and punishment. Indeed, it would be difficult to exaggerate the extent of the modern State's power, influence and control.

We are now so familiar and accepting of the State's pre-eminence in all things, that few think to question it. Though ideologies of the Right which expressly idolize the State and its leaders in the way that Fascism does are generally objects of derision and denunciation, there is no shortage of political philosophies whose tacit effect is to sanction it. For the most part, the left/liberal and centrist political creeds of the present, and the political parties that give expression to them, concur in their belief that the State both is and should be always with us. They disagree only in how and to what ends its powers are to be used. Should the State own or merely regulate the means of production and the infrastructure of transportation? Should the State privatize some of its essential functions — prisons for instance — or run them directly? Should health and education be supplied directly or indirectly by the State? And so on. Even new self styled 'radical' movements look to the State to effect their radicalism. Feminism has sought legal proscription and State-backed affirmative action programmes to address what it sees to be the patriarchal inheritance of the past. Likewise, it is the State that 'Green' parties and pressure groups chiefly seek to influence and the international collaboration of States in which they place their hopes of avoiding the various environmental catastrophes they predict.

In short, every contemporary political movement sees the State as the principal, often the sole, instrument of realizing its ambitions. Even more importantly for my purposes, all such movements subscribe to, and reflect, a widespread and unquestioning acceptance of the idea that however extended the modern State becomes, its excesses can be checked and its actions can be sanctioned (it might not be fanciful to say 'sanctified') by democracy, that where the State has the support of 'the will of the people' it is thereby justified in all its operations. Accordingly, their task, if they are not to take to the bomb and the barricade, is to secure control of the State (or at least to influence it) through the democratic process. Having done so, they can claim justification in using the resources, power and authority of the State to implement the policies they favour.

The principal aim of this book is to question this assumption — that democratic endorsement legitimizes the modern State. However, since this immediately raises the question 'Why does the State *need* legitimation?' a second aim is to show that the State as we know it requires justification, a justification that, as we shall see, it is not specially easy to supply. Together these aims may be interpreted as an attempt to make the case against the democratic State. This is a difficult thing to do for at least three reasons.

First, the legitimacy of the democratic State is deeply embedded in our ways of thinking. It pervades almost all that is said and thought and done in contemporary political life. The assumption that we need the State is so much taken for granted, it is hard to get doubts about its legitimacy taken seriously, and the word 'democratic' has such a powerful positive connotation that questioning it is like questioning the desirability of social justice or a healthy life-style.

Second, anyone who raises questions as fundamental as those I want to raise is quickly cast into some preconceived political 'position'. To make the case I want to make I have to elaborate and endorse anti-democratic arguments, and to give considerable credence to the merits of anarchism, strictly understood. To describe my aim in this way, however, is to invite not only misunderstanding but ridicule. Anarchists are black coated bomb throwers, are they not, or hooligans who organize riots at international meetings of government ministers. Anti-democrats are right-wing reactionaries, who have some kind of emotional hang-up about empire and monarchy and think that everything went to the dogs when ordinary people ceased to be kept in their place. That some of the people who hold these views are often labelled anarchist and anti-democrat (by themselves as well as other), is not something I could or would deny. On the other hand, to identify every criticism of the democratic State with one of these camps, or even worse some unimaginably unholy alliance of the two, is to ignore genuine lines of thought that are crucial to understanding contemporary political culture. Blackening the opposition may be an attractive strategy. Anti-democratic arguments, and defences of anarchism, are highly uncomfortable for the self-image of the contemporary Western world. The technique of argument by innuendo, however, hardly accords with the exercise of reason and pursuit of genuine enlightenment that is an equally important part of that self-image. If the democratic State is as admirable as most people suppose, it should be a relatively easy matter to explain the characteristics that make it so.

The third obstacle in the way of taking seriously the kind of criticisms I mean to explore is that they seem deeply impractical, of purely 'academic' interest in the bad sense. This is an objection I have myself brought against anarchism elsewhere (see Graham (a) Chp 9). The fact is that the democratic State is here to stay for any foreseeable future. To suggest that it ought to be abolished or even that it ought to be less democratic — if these are indeed amongst the conclusions sustained by the line of argument I mean to explore — has all the defects of a council of perfection; it simply isn't going to happen, and people who advocate such a policy thereby relegate themselves to the ranks of the politically irrelevant. It is possible to reply to this charge that, faced with the inevitable, there is still something to be said for not going gently into the dark night but raging against the dying of the light. Why, though, induce in oneself a wholly futile rage? For my own part I think this third objection to the enterprise I have set myself is a most important one, and in the closing chapter I shall attempt to face it and answer it as honestly as I can. But there is little point in addressing this issue unless it can be shown that the arguments against the democratic State are powerful ones, arguments that it is hard simply to ignore. For this reason, I shall suspend the question of practicality for the moment and try in the next few chapters to show that the supporter of the democratic State has some very serious questions to answer.

One further point is in order. What I am engaged in here is political philosophy in the European tradition. It is a subject I have studied and taught for years, and anything I have to say is both formed by and deeply indebted to that tradition. At the same time, the aim of this essay is cultural criticism, and it will have failed if it engages only with political philosophers. In an attempt to reach the wide audience that an essay in cultural criticism requires, I have striven to write in a manner accessible to anyone interested in careful reflection on the world in which we live, and accordingly I have dispensed with the usual apparatus of the academic book, chiefly citations, cross-references and footnotes. From time to time I shall mention and discuss some of the 'big' names — Plato, Hobbes, Locke, Marx, Mill and so on — but I have made no effort to engage directly with the large and professional literature of contemporary political philosophy. Many of the issues that concern modern political philosophers are indeed dealt with here, but in such a way, I hope, that anyone unfamiliar with or indifferent to scholarly books and journals will be able to follow. The point is to engage minds in reflection and debate, not to inform them about political philosophy or its history.

CHAPTER 1

Leviathan

Leviathan is the name of a sea-monster that makes an appearance in the Psalms — 'there go the ships, and there is that leviathan whom thou made to take his pastime therein' (Ps. 104:26). It is also the title of the greatest work of political philosophy in the English language. Published by Thomas Hobbes (1588–1679) in 1651, *Leviathan* aims to deduce the necessity of the sovereign State from first principles with the same rigour and precision that theorems are derived from axioms in geometry. Here the name refers to the State — 'that mortal god, to which we owe . . . our peace and defence', and it is part of my purpose to ask whether in this connection also, Leviathan is not the name of a monster.

Probably no one, apart from Hobbes himself, has ever been persuaded that the geometrical deduction succeeds, but there is no denying *Leviathan's* exhilarating intellectual ambition, the subtlety of its argument and the power of its prose. My aim in this chapter is to present the case against, and to show as convincingly as I can, that there are powerful reasons to deny not just the necessity of the State, but its desirability. These reasons may not prove conclusive, but they are weighty enough to cause us to think much more carefully than we usually do about the State. Furthermore, they enable us to identify the point on which the defence of democracy turns. I shall argue that our faith in democracy rests crucially upon the belief that it can save us from the worst ravages of the State. Subsequent chapters will then explore the question of whether it can. First, though, I need to show that the State is an institution sorely in need of defence, and to ensure that in arguing about the State we are all arguing about the same thing we must start with a definition and some distinctions.

The Definition of the State

The first distinction to be made is that between society and the State. Despite the fact that these two terms are commonly used interchangeably, it is a serious mistake to confuse them. While the State is unquestionably the single most significant institution in almost every contemporary society, it is nonetheless only one amongst many. With the exception of extraordinary aberrations like North Korea and the Cambodia of Pol Pot, all societies include commercial, industrial and voluntary corporate entities that are in varying degrees independent of the State. The State is special, certainly, but it is not all inclusive. Though families, businesses, churches and charities are not departments of State, they are as much part of the fabric of society as it is. What then distinguishes the State from these other institutions and organizations? I shall define its essential character in this way: the State is the monopolist of legitimate coercion.

Each part of this definition is important. 'Coercion' means forcing people to do things. We can force people to do things by means of threat of penalty or violence, or by direct physical, social and psychological compulsion and constraint. The use of such means is not confined to the State, of course. Thieves, bandits, and gangsters of various sorts, all of whom use coercion in pursuit of their activities, are a familiar part of human experience. What marks off the police from the Mafia, however, is the claim of the former to *legitimacy*. The difference can be brought into sharp focus by thinking about the distinction between a fine and a theft. When the Mafia take my money away, it is theft; when the police take my money away, it is a fine. Both involve seizing my possessions forcibly, but while a theft is unlawful, a fine is lawful.

'By whose law?' it might be asked. Strictly, since a Mafia might be run in accordance with a tacit 'code of conduct' or even have declared and acknowledged rules of a quasi-legal nature, what is at issue is not so much lawfulness as legitimacy. The State claims legitimacy for its coercive actions, a legitimacy that everyone would deny to the Mafia or other groups of criminals, however extensive, well-organized or rule-governed they may be. Despite the fact that at one level their activities will bear a similar description, the police are not engaged in a protection racket, even though the protection they offer comes at a price forcibly extracted in the form of taxes. This, at any rate, is what the conception of the State as a legitimate user of coercion implies.

Furthermore, the State claims a *monopoly* on legitimate coercion, a claim revealed in the fact that other institutions can use coercion only while, and to the extent that, the State permits them to do so. Families and schools, for instance, may use corporal punishment or physical constraint, but the extent to which they are allowed to is determined by the State through its laws and regulatory powers. The State can, and in many places nowadays does, forbid parents to use physical coercion in the rearing of their children, and prohibit or confine the steps that teachers may take in the disciplining of their pupils. Importantly, this relationship runs only one way. Neither parents nor schools can set limits to the coercive powers of the State. In fact, *no* other organization or institution can. This is what it means to say that the State claims a monopoly on legitimate coercion, and the question thus arises as to whether there is or is not good reason to have, or at least endorse, such an institution.

Limited, Unlimited and Totalitarian States

The definition of the State as the monopolist of legitimate coercion neatly captures its essential characteristic, and is useful for analytical purposes. But it easily gives rise to misunderstanding. We ought not to suppose that the State so defined is necessarily totalitarian. There is an important distinction to be drawn between limited and unlimited States, and it is only the latter that we have reason to describe as totalitarian. Even here there is scope for further misunderstanding. Though everyday speech carries this implication, to describe a State as totalitarian is not necessarily the same as declaring it oppressive. Some explanation of these distinctions is a crucial preliminary to the question of its desirability.

A limited State is one the range of whose actions is constitutionally confined or restricted. The classic example is the United States. The Constitution of the US incorporates an important restriction on what the State may and may not do. Famously, it may not use its coercive powers in the promotion of any one religion. By contrast, the British State is an *unlimited* one (though since its entry to the EU the European Courts now constitute something of a limit). That is to say, there are no restrictions on what the British Parliament may legislate about, including even, the form of prayer that is to be used in public worship.

In this rather special sense, the British State is totalitarian; there is nothing to which it may not turn its attention and no aspect of the life of its citizens that it may not use its coercive powers to regulate. Yet despite this description, it is obvious, I think, that the British State is not an especially oppressive one. On the contrary, there is much to be said for the view that Britain is a model of civil peace and personal liberty compared with many, perhaps most other, societies — even though the State that governs it is unlimited, and in this sense totalitarian. The point of comparison with the US, then, is not the degree of oppressiveness, but the scope of its power and authority. The powers of the British State may be unlimited, but it does not follow, and is not the case, that they actually obtrude into every aspect of its citizens' lives. In order to mark this distinction, and in line with common usage, I shall reserve the term 'totalitarian State' for those instances in which the State is not merely constitutionally unlimited, but strikingly obtrusive and oppressive in practice.

Actually, totalitarian States, so conceived, need not be unlimited. Some States that have constitutional limits can operate within those limits in grossly oppressive ways. This is true of many of the States that emerged from colonial Africa; the limits built into their constitutions have often proved a poor defence against corruption and brutality. Such States may be contrasted with more 'liberal' States that accord to their citizens a far greater degree of personal freedom. The distinctions between limited/unlimited and liberal/totalitarian, then, do not coincide. This is a point worth stressing because the case against the democratic State that is most worth considering is *not* a case confined to the totalitarian State. Objections to totalitarianism are easily formulated, but just for that reason they do not have any special interest. Similarly, constitutional arguments that favour limited over unlimited States are too familiar to be specially interesting. The interesting case, rather, is against *the State as such*, which is to say, against any institution, limited or unlimited, totalitarian or liberal, that claims a monopoly on the legitimate use of coercion.

Law, Trust and Social Co-ordination

On what basis is such a case to be constructed? There is a question here as to where the burden of proof lies. Should we take the existence of the State to be in some sense 'natural' to human society, the 'default position' as it were? Or are we to think of the State as an artificial construct whose rationale needs to be explained? One of the attractions of Hobbes's *Leviathan* is that it seems to combine these alternatives by showing that the State is something that inevitably arises from the natural condition in which people find themselves.

How so? The most famous passage in Hobbes's *Leviathan* is that in which he describes a world without a State as a 'war of everyone against everyone' the result of which is

> No arts; no letters; no society; and which is worst of all, continual fear and danger of violent death; and the life of man, solitary, poor, nasty, brutish and short (Hobbes, p. 82: for references see bibliography).

The life of man, solitary, poor, nasty, brutish and short; this is a dismal prospect, and anyone convinced of its inevitability in a world without a State, is sure to be persuaded of the State's necessity. Now it is important to ask, as many of Hobbes's contemporaries asked, whether his description of the world without the State is well founded. What reason do we have to think that, if the State did not exist, a war of everyone against everyone would indeed break out? Hobbes's own reason for drawing this conclusion derives from his account of what motivates human beings, his understanding of human psychology in short, an understanding in which personal desire and the love of glory figure prominently. Other writers took a more optimistic view. Hobbes's contemporary, the German legal theorist Samuel Pufendorff (1632–94) for instance, drew attention to the fact that people naturally form families, with the result that egoistic inclinations are generally tempered by ties of affection to others. Bishop Joseph Butler (1692–1752) in his celebrated *Sermons* (1726) identified benevolence towards other people as one of the two basic human motivations.

So we need not share Hobbes's pessimistic view of human nature, but to argue with him on this score is not a very promising tactic. If people cannot agree about the desirability of the State, they are even less likely to agree on the topic of human nature. This is because just how we are to determine what is and is not basic to human nature is a very difficult matter. It seems equally easy to assert and to deny that human nature is this way or that. Moreover, to the modern mind the very concept of human nature sounds dated (though to a degree the sociobiology inspired by E.O. Wilson has done something to revive it). The rise of anthropology has led many people to deny that there *is* any one human nature underlying the disparate social and cultural forms in which human beings are to be found. Accordingly, undermining Hobbes's defence of the State by undermining the picture of human psychology on which it rests is not so easy, and made harder by the fact that, in so far as people are prepared to speculate about human nature at all, they are inclined to find the attribution of a basically egoistic motivation rather plausible.

How then might we challenge Hobbes's defence of Leviathan? One answer lies in rehearsing some simple facts about social order, facts which support the contention that it does not actually rely so very much on the enforcement of law. The key to effective social life is social co-ordination, which is to say, the presence of various devices and strategies by which the differing and sometimes competing desires of individuals can be co-ordinated without conflict. Consider, in this regard, the simple device of the queue, of waiting in line. The remarkable efficacy of this device for social co-ordination can be witnessed any day in the supermarket. There, as in countless other places, individuals pursue their particular desires for goods and services, desires that differ from each other, may be in competition, and can potentially lead to conflict. Yet, while fighting does occasionally break out between people waiting in line, and while acute shortages can produce rioting and looting, in the vast majority of instances, the device of the queue is quite remarkably effective in securing good social order in the satisfaction of individual purposes.

This is one striking device, but there are other phenomena of equal importance — mutual trust, for example. When I leave my goods to be repaired I generally trust that the repairer is *bona fide*, just as he or she trusts that I will return for my goods and pay for the repair that has been carried out on them. Trust, as a matter of fact, underlies a vast deal of what we do. I stop to ask directions of a stranger, for example, and take it on trust that I am not being mischievously pointed in the wrong direction. I go to the doctor and trust that the advice and treatment I am given arises from real knowledge and a genuine intention to cure. I order goods to be delivered and trustingly take a day off work in the belief that the delivery will be made as promised.

Now of course it is true that these things can go wrong. There are occasional queue jumpers, bogus tradesmen, bad doctors, and people wait for deliveries in vain. My trust is not always well placed, with the result that one argument for thinking we need an institution like the coercive State is that we have to have legal enforcement in the background for the occasions on which trust breaks down. Moreover, or so the defender of the State might claim, it is the knowledge of the ever present possibility of recourse to law that sustains the general atmosphere of trust. In other words, it is the knowledge that we *could* take steps to ensure that those with whom we have dealings do what they say they will do, and take their turn like everyone else, that generates and sustains non-legal patterns of social co-ordination.

This is a line of argument that is invoked very widely, it seems to me. Without any of the psychological picture that Hobbes so carefully constructs, a great many people will argue that we *have* to have the State because otherwise social conflict, if not social chaos, would prevail. Is this true? In my view there are several reasons to think that it is not.

First, it does not take much reflection to see that if the organization of supermarkets were constantly on the edge of disruption, the officers of the State — i.e. the police — could do little to counteract this. It simply is not plausible (because not feasible) to suppose that police, even in considerable numbers, could enforce the sort of order that is required for a large and busy supermarket to function effectively, never mind the thousands upon thousands of these that many modern societies support. We know very well that when rioting does break out, it can be difficult for well armed and trained police in sizeable numbers to control a mob in even one small locality.

Second, it seems to me fanciful to think that what stops most people queue jumping, deceiving strangers, or conning customers, is the thought that they will get caught and punished. There are a number of observations worth making on this point. Speaking for myself, the reason I do not go in for murder and mayhem is that I have no inclination to do so, and many better, more profitable and more enjoyable ways of spending my time. I imagine this to be the case with the vast majority of my acquaintances. Of how many people is it true that they have a powerful inclination to anti-social behaviour, an inclination that is checked only by the fear of punishment? Not many, I am inclined to think. And if I did feel inclined to fraud, theft or burglary, then it would be irrational on my part to be deterred by the thought of being caught and punished. This is because the chances of its happening are very small. In a well ordered, peaceable and generally law abiding society such as contemporary Britain, for example, the clear up rate for all crimes is currently 6%. That is to say, if you commit a crime, the chances of getting away with it are better than 90%. This 6% rate is an average. The clear up rate for violent crimes against the person is very much higher, but it is offset by the clear up rates for petty theft, credit card fraud, and minor burglary which for all practical purposes are effectively zero. Anyone who is deterred from petty theft solely by the thought that they might get caught can rationally go ahead with impunity.

Third, we know that where trust breaks down, or at least is seriously undermined, recourse to law — litigation — is a very imperfect remedy, and generally serves to make matters worse. Recently, this has become a theme taken up by a number of writers (Onara O'Neill in her 2002 Reith Lectures is a notable example), who have argued convincingly to my mind that the general shift from a culture of trust to a culture of accountability such as has been witnessed in changing Western political and social mores, has led to more and not less tension and strife between members of the same society. The move in health and education, for instance, from a unspecified conception of professional pride and responsibility to quasi-legal codes of conduct enforcible by regulatory bodies, has for the most part diminished the confidence with which ordinary people enter hospital or commit their children to the care of schools. The more we perceive a need for the State to hold people legally accountable, the less we place our trust in them.

The fourth point to be made against the defence of the State that we are here considering is perhaps the most telling. The existence of the State does *not* put an end to criminal activity. Theft of property, fraudulent transactions, kidnapping, violence against the person and so on, all occur in societies with a strong and efficient State. This observation is specially worth making because there is a tendency among those who argue for the necessity of the State as a defence against lawlessness to suppose that, while without a State lawlessness would be major problem, its existence more or less solves that problem. It is illegitimate to reason in this way, however, because it effectively compares a perfectly functioning State with a radically dysfunctional stateless society. To get the proper measure of the argument we have to compare like with like — either the imperfectly functioning State with imperfectly functioning statelessness, or the perfectly functioning State with a perfectly functioning anarchy.

Of course, the defender of the State is likely to claim that there is no such thing as a perfectly functioning anarchy, or if there is, its 'perfect' functioning is precisely one of chaos and conflict. But if we mean by 'anarchy' what the word literally means — no State — we have evidence to the contrary. There have been until very recently stateless societies — the nomadic tribes of East Africa and North America for instance — and careful studies of them have revealed that, in general, they have far lower levels of anti-social behaviour than modern societies with States. The people in societies without States are generally social conformists. The position is complicated by size, of course. These stateless societies have all been small to the point where most relationships within them are personal; by contrast modern Western societies are large and for the most part involve relationships between strangers. Respective size, however, is not entirely relevant here. The point rather is that the absence of a State does not automatically mean social chaos, and the presence of a State does not necessarily secure low levels of anti-social behaviour. Just how effective any given State is in this regard, and just how life in a stateless society works out, are both empirical matters. We cannot reason a priori here, and this means that the defender of the State cannot claim that the absence of the State will inevitably lead to radical social disorder.

There is, I think, a real question about the possibility of a large stateless society. Part of the problem is not so much its internal ability to function, but its defence against external threats from societies *with* States. While the nomadic Zande or Nuer do not present any significant opportunity for the States that surround them (though even they have now been taken over), a much larger, richer society would prove an attractive target, and an anarchical society would, by definition, have no State to protect it from the incursions of others. For this reason, perhaps, anarchy really is an impossible ideal, and one that ultimately we cannot defend to any point or purpose. However, the theoretical possibility is enough to show that the question before us is whether the State, if it is not positively beneficial, is a *necessary* evil, or just an unavoidable one.

Estimating the Benefits of Statehood

The upshot is this. The argument we have been considering casts its defence of the State in terms of the prevention of harm. The import of the points I have made in response is that this is a *relative* judgement between good and less good, not an absolute judgement between good and bad. Such a judgement must turn on empirical evidence and the balance of probabilities. The most the defender of the State is entitled to claim is that the existence of a State is likely to secure a lower level of anti-social behaviour than would otherwise be the case. Is this true?

To repeat: there is no room for a priori reasoning here. Many people faced with this question are tempted to say 'It's bound to', but in fact whether it does or not is an empirical question, and hence whether it is likely to or not is an empirical question also. How might we gather the evidence that would allow us to take a view one way or the other? Difficult though this might appear to be, we can throw some light on the question by reflecting both on possibilities and experiences.

First, if the State is an instrument for good, it can also be an instrument for harm. The very feature of the modern State which makes it a powerful counter to lawlessness and anti-social behaviour — its social pre-eminence as the monopolist of legitimate coercion — makes it an equally powerful — and attractive — agent of partisanship and corruption. This is a possibility that the historical experience of the twentieth century puts in a very vivid light, and one that only gross insensibility to political realities could make us regard with anything but anxiety. If the State had not existed, the ghastly ravages of Stalin, Hitler, Mao, and Pol Pot could not have assumed the proportions they did. It is only thanks to the existence, organization and efficiency, but above all authority and power, of the State that the genocide of Ukrainians and Jews, the Cultural Revolution, and Year Zero could be both contemplated and to a horrifying extent realized. Anti-social behaviour of the sort the State is intended to prevent or even eliminate is objectionable because it harms people badly; but the scale of the harm pales to insignificance beside the scale of harm that can and has been brought about by the State gone wrong. 'That mortal god, to which we owe . . . our peace and defence' can also be a monster from whom nothing is safe and to whom nothing is holy. In naming it 'Leviathan', Hobbes may have unwittingly captured more of its character than he meant.

By the same token, of course, a weak State may be correspondingly harmless. When in times past the power of kings to check disobedient or intransigent subjects was severely limited, so too was their power to cause mayhem on their own account. And even the best established of States can fall into the hands of madmen; witness the Emperor Caligula or Idi Amin. In these cases we should fear the existence of an effective and authoritative State, and in the light of their possibility view the consequentialist defence of the State with appropriate caution. In a stateless society there is a limit to the harm the power-crazed can do. In a society with a State, they have greatly increased scope for the exercise of their manic aspirations.

These are of course extreme cases. Most States at most times have come nowhere near committing the savage excesses of the Nazis or the Communists, and most Heads of State are models of sanity compared with Caligula. Or so it seems reasonable to suppose. Yet even if this is true, there are qualifications to be made such as must leave us wondering whether the State may not cause more harm than it prevents in much more modest ways. This possibility arises because the law itself may inadvertently engineer new and harmful levels of criminality. One of the most telling examples of this is Prohibition in the United States of America. The authority and the power of the Federal Government to make the sale and consumption of alcohol illegal called into existence a network of organized crime that continued to wreak damage years after Prohibition was ended. Arguably indeed, this exercise of State power gave organized crime a fillip that it would never otherwise have had, and thereby assisted rather than retarded the levels of anti-social behaviour of which the theory of the State makes so much.

Prohibition is a thing of the past, but in my view precisely the same point can be made with respect to the policy of most contemporary States on drugs such as cannabis, cocaine and heroin. The so-called 'war on drugs' has been lost at vast expense for many decades, and this is largely because its basic cause is their illegality. The State, in fact, has called into existence the very thing it is at war with — a class of anti-social behaviour whose anti-social character is not intrinsic to its nature but rather a result of its having been so declared. I have set out the detailed support of this contention elsewhere and will not repeat it now (see Whynes and Bean, ch. 13). Suffice to note how strange it is that a world that has had the experience of Prohibition to learn from should make exactly the same mistake with a different set of recreational drugs.

Both Prohibition and the contemporary policy on drugs show that social causality is complex, and the impact of State actions is part of this complexity. To suppose that whatever the State declares to be crime is seriously anti-social, and that its making this declaration puts an end to the behaviour in question, is naïve to the point of irresponsibility. Societies and human beings simply do not work in this straightforward way, and because they do not, we have reason to be careful about the benefits we attribute to the existence of the State even in contexts far less dramatically destructive than those of Nazi Germany and Communist Russia.

It follows that any judgement about the State's desirability based upon the consequences of its existence for good and ill must at best be very uncertain. While there may be reason to suppose with Hobbes that Leviathan can be the institution to which we owe our peace and defence, historical experience shows that it can also be the institution from which we have most to fear. There is, however, another line of thought, also owing to Hobbes, which can be invoked in the State's defence. This turns on the idea that there are special but important circumstances in which the good of society as a whole requires the existence of a coercive authority.

General Good *versus* Individual Advantage

Consider the following circumstance. A lakeside community derives its livelihood from fishing, but the stocks of fish in the lake are declining. To preserve stocks in the longer term to the benefit of all, it seems that the only remedy is individual quotas, which is to say a limit on how many fish each fisherman may take from the lake. This way the future of everyone will be secured. The alternative is that the community as a whole falls into economic decline. However, despite the fact that quotas are clearly to the general good, there is a pattern of reasoning which sets the individual at odds with this desirable goal. An individual fisherman can reason cogently in the following way.

> Suppose that *I* stick to my quota, but others do not. In this case, the lake will get fished out, and everyone will be a loser in the long term. But I will be a loser in the short term as well, since by confining myself to the quota allocated to me I will suffer an immediate drop in income that others do not. Suppose on the other hand that I *break* my quota. Then, if others break theirs, the lake gets fished out, certainly, but I am not a special loser. Contrariwise, if others keep to their quotas while I break mine, the fish stocks will be preserved to my long term benefit as well as theirs, but unlike them, I will not suffer an immediate drop in income either. So, whether other fishermen ignore *or* observe their quotas, my best strategy is to ignore mine.

This line of reasoning is perfectly cogent in itself. It just is true that in the circumstances described it is in the interests of the individual to break the rules. The problem, of course, is that *every* individual fisherman can reason in this way with equal cogency, so that no one has a reason to keep the quota. But in that case the collapse of the fishing stock is guaranteed. If everyone looks rationally to his own interests, then the interests of all are sacrificed. How is this paradox to be overcome?

One answer, very much in the spirit of Hobbes, is that it is precisely in these circumstances that a political authority with coercive powers is required. It will be in the interests of each individual fisherman to keep to the rules if (a) every one else does and (b) he will suffer if he does not. If the chain of individualistic reason that has such a destructive effect on the general good is to be broken, individuals have to know how others will behave. Now they can only know that everyone *will* comply with the quotas if they know that everyone will be *compelled* to, and it is here that we find a real argument for the necessity of the State as a monopolist of legitimate coercion. Such an institution is needed to ensure that the potential conflict between individual rationality and the common good is overcome.

This is I think a plausible argument, even a powerful one. It shows that, since human beings in society can act in ways that are individually rational but socially destructive, and thus highly detrimental to all, societies need an institution in which coercion can be used to advance and protect the general good, a general good that is in the longer-term interests of everyone. The same argument can be given a further twist. It is not simply that individuals need to know that others will be compelled to comply with the rules that are in the general interest. It is also the case that human beings have a strong sense of justice and fairness, and will expect those who uphold the rules by obeying them to be vindicated by the due punishment of those who break them. It is partly along these lines that John Locke (1632–1704) defends the State. But though plausible, the argument is far from conclusive. We might note for a start that if the compliance problem arises within stateless societies, it also arises in the *international* society of States (as the European Common Agricultural Policy has often demonstrated) with the result that it seems in the end to be an argument for a World Superstate rather than for the Nation State as we know it. Secondly, if we think we have good reason to predict that the State will do more harm than good, then this will cancel out the conclusion of the compliance problem on the grounds that the solution is more costly than the problem to which it is the solution.

A middle position, however, would appear to be this. The compliance argument gives us reason to accept the State as a potentially valuable institution. Such an institution can of course be misused, and thus work *against* the best interests of all. However, this possibility does not count against the State as such. It implies, rather, that in and of itself the State is neutral — neither a good thing nor a bad. If so, it follows that the deep reservations about the State rehearsed in an earlier section — the excesses of Stalin, Hitler and so on — are not entirely to the point. It is not the State, but those in charge of it, who should be the objects of our anxiety. In short it is the *Government* around which safeguards need to be set.

It is with this shift of focus from State to government that we find the connection between the issues discussed so far and the democratic ideal I want to examine critically. According to this ideal, precisely because the State presents a potential threat rather than a benefit to those who are subject to it, it needs to be set around with and subject to democratic safeguards. It is democracy that ensures, or at least is the best way of ensuring, that the government which controls the State reflects the beliefs and opinions of society at large and thus pursues policies that are genuinely in accordance with the general interest and the will of the people.

This is an attractive line of thought. Indeed, in my estimation it is belief in the cogency of this line of thought (a belief more often assumed than expressed) that sustains our faith in the democratic State. This faith has two elements. It holds, first that we need the State for the promotion and protection of justice and the general good, and second, that we need democracy to make sure its operation really is in accordance with that good and that those who run it are accountable to the people they govern.

My question is whether our faith in the democratic State is well founded. This is the issue to be explored at length in later chapters. But for the moment we should note an important presupposition that often sustains it — that *good* government and *democratic* government pretty much come to the same thing. This identification begs the question. The expressions 'democratic government' and 'good government' do not have the same meaning. To suppose that they do, is to make the merits of democracy tautological — true by definition — and this they cannot be. In *The Republic* and elsewhere Plato raises important doubts about Athenian democracy, and for the larger part of European history the majority of people have believed that democracy is a dangerous and defective form of government. This belief may be mistaken, and Plato's arguments may in the end prove invalid, but they are not meaningless. To *assume* that *democratic* government is automatically *good* government is to settle debate by linguistic stipulation. Plato's challenge, I hope to show, is a real one, whatever our final estimation of its worth may be. A necessary condition of appreciating its strength lies in acknowledging that democracy is only one possible form of government among others, and must therefore establish its credentials like any other.

To the contemporary mind, of course, it has long since done so. The superiority of democracy over all other forms of government is so deeply ingrained in our way of thinking that alternatives such as meritocracy (government by the most able) or plutocracy (government by those with the largest social stake) say, can be declared imperfect without argument or evidence, as though they were all primitive forms of tribalism or manifestations of class-ridden inequalities. In this way, very often, democracy wins by default because it is deemed to have no real contenders. One of my main contentions in this essay is that if we can persuade ourselves to take the matter seriously, we shall discover that there are good arguments and substantial evidence *against* democracy (whatever weight we might ultimately attribute to them). The almost total failure even to consider them has made our faith in democracy blind. And blind faith is no better a base for democracy that it is for fascism or communism.

Summary

The point we have reached is this. Purely consequential arguments in favour of the State, defined as an institution possessing a monopoly on the use of legitimate coercion, are likely to be inconclusive. This is because they are empirical in nature and given the number of different States there have been and the length of time they have been in existence, all the relevant facts would be difficult to gather and assess. People generally get round this difficulty by *assuming* that if the State did not exist, the level of anti-social behaviour would be intolerable, that human harm and social chaos would be everywhere. But we cannot declare this to be the case *a priori*, because in the light of such knowledge as we have, it is far from obvious. We know, for example, that there have been stateless societies in which social conformity is the norm. Even if we agree that no large modern society could be stateless, we know that most social intercourse takes place quite satisfactorily without recourse to the police and the courts, and if it did not there is little that the State could do about it. Conversely, criminological surveys tell us that in many modern societies where the State is pre-eminent, there are high levels of crime, and that the State prisons whose purpose is to check these levels more often than not exacerbate them.

Much more strikingly, while in theory it is the role of the State to ameliorate the horrors of the Hobbesian war of all against all, in practice the State can become a major source of violence against those subject to it. Not infrequently both the apparatus and the authority of the State has been used as the means by which the property and livelihood of some people is corruptly and arbitrarily appropriated by others. This is a depressingly recurrent feature of the history of the State, in fact, and something that happened on a gigantic scale in Nazi Germany, Communist China and the Soviet Union. Yet these are only some of many instances in the twentieth century and must give serious pause to any unthinking advocacy of the desirability of the State.

Even in less dramatically horrible cases, the activities of the State can be an important stimulus to criminality. Prohibition in the US and the policy of most contemporary States on drugs provide good examples. The power to declare actions illegal and to threaten punishment is not confined to murder, theft, rape and so on. The State can force much less objectionable aspects of human conduct into the hands of those who are prepared to use criminal methods in pursuit of profit, and when it does so, it becomes a major cause of the very thing it is supposed to cure.

Still, the claim that consequential arguments about the role and efficacy of the State are inevitably inconclusive works both ways. If we cannot declare the State to be an unqualified agent for good, we cannot declare it to be an inevitable source of harm either. We thus need some other argument to break the deadlock, and there is indeed an alternative line of thought to which the proponent of the State can appeal. This consists in drawing attention to circumstances in which there is a genuine conflict between the general good and advantage to the individual, the sort of circumstance illustrated by the example of declining fish stocks. Here, it seems, we can discern the need for an institution with powers of coercion that will make it rational for individuals to act in ways that accord with the interests of all, and will apply appropriate standards of justice and fairness.

Let us agree that this is a convincing argument in favour of the State. Even so, earlier doubts have not gone away. Ought we not to engage in a measure of cost benefit analysis and ask whether the unquestionable advantage of the State in the circumstances described is not offset by its potential to turn into a source of harm and destruction? One reply is this. Perhaps we cannot construct an adequate justification for the State in all its forms. But we can do so where the form of the State includes safeguards against its abuse. Chief among these safeguards are the provisions of democracy. Consequently, the State that *can* be justified is the democratic State. This brings us to the next chapter.

CHAPTER 2

Politics and Reason

If we are to consider the merits of the democratic State dispassion-
ately, bearing in mind the existence of alternatives (in history and in
theory if not in practice) then we must begin by characterizing it in a
non-contentious way. This is relatively easy conceptually speaking,
but not so easy to accomplish rhetorically. So strong is the tendency
to identify democratic government with good government, that
faced with objections to democracy, its advocates are likely to
respond by changing the definition. So, for instance, it is common for
the problem known as 'the tyranny of the majority' (about which I
shall have more to say later) to meet with the reply 'that's not what I
mean by democracy'. The definition of democracy is not indefinitely
malleable, however. There are, as it seems to me, three indispensable
elements. These are the sovereignty of the people, universal suffrage
and majority rule. We can see that these are indeed essential compo-
nents by imagining a political system in which they are absent. However peaceful and prosperous a society may be, however benign its
government, and whatever the rights it may bestow upon its citizens, if it is one in which no elections involving the general public are
held, where political offices are closed to all but a relatively small
elite, and where political decisions lie ultimately in the hands of a
single supreme ruler, it cannot be called democratic.

This is, in fact, the sort of society that Plato defends in *The Republic*
and he defends it expressly against the democratic regime that oper-
ated in Athens. In many minds, no doubt, there lurks the vague idea
that, since ancient Athens was the birthplace of democracy, and
Plato its most famous philosopher, Plato's Republic must be a
democracy. Nothing could be further from the truth. In the *Republic*
and elsewhere (notably the dialogue *Gorgias*) Plato argues vigor-
ously against Athenian democracy and in favour of the idea that a
well-ordered society is one in which absolute rule is enjoyed by peo-

ple specially trained to exercise it — the philosophers — and where everyone else is accorded, and confined to, the place that the philosophers know it would be best for them to occupy.

Now no one today could take this proposal seriously, and in so far as they did, it would be to excoriate it as some vile form of fascism. (In 1959 the British politician Richard Crossman published a well-known book entitled *Plato Today* in which he claimed just this). Yet, as I hope to show, aspects of Plato's argument still present us with a challenge, and what is more, a challenge that it takes some ingenuity to respond to. To dispel one possible misunderstanding right from the outset, however, let me say immediately that I take it to be an incontestable truth that there is no social group, to be distinguished by history, race, gender or economic status, that is 'naturally' fitted to government. It is no part of my purpose to defend the idea that government should be confined to such a group. What I do think, though, is that Plato's attack on democracy does bear meaningfully on what is generally taken to be the moral basis of democracy, namely an egalitarian conception of the sovereignty of the people. Such a conception came to prominence long after Plato, of course, but it is susceptible to Plato's basic critique, that democracy is a profoundly irrational form of government. It is this alleged conflict between democracy and rationality that provides the subject of this chapter.

Plato's Challenge

The democracy Plato attacked was significantly different to the democracies of today. For a start, it came nowhere near universal suffrage since large numbers of the people subject to the decisions of the Athenian assembly had no part in making them — women and slaves, for example. But what Plato objects to is a system in which, far from being the necessary conditions of participation that they ought to be, knowledge and competence are not factors at all. Using an analogy which has been deployed by political thinkers ever since, Plato contends that giving control of the ship of State to all and sundry is no more rational than putting a newly recruited rating on the same footing as the master mariner. Now this parallel can be applied to a large or small number. The point is that within the assembly, one voice is as good as another because one vote is as good as another. And Plato thinks it manifestly foolish to entrust the government of the State to those who have no special knowledge or expertise in running it.

His objection, in fact, has two dimensions to it. First, he thinks it intrinsically wrong to sanction and encourage inexpert action. Second he thinks that by doing so democracy encourages demagoguery since it is those who are able to sway the multitude who will be able to command the majority. These two points are related, and it is easiest to show their relation by expanding a little on the context in which Plato is writing.

Plato was engaged in a protracted dispute with the Sophists. The Sophists, at least as he represents them, were teachers of rhetoric or public speaking, and they generally subscribed to the view that matters of right and wrong are matters of conventional opinion, in contrast to the demonstrable truths of science and mathematics. The aim of the rhetorician as opposed to the philosopher, accordingly, was not to *prove*, but to *persuade*, and by learning how to speak powerfully and convincingly, a politician could persuade enough people to share his opinion to make it prevail. This, on their view, was the value of rhetoric.

Elements of this dispute linger in our language. To describe an argument as sophistical is to deem it more impressive in appearance than substance. More importantly, the philosophical position occupied by the Sophists is alive and well within contemporary culture. Very large numbers of people, probably the great majority, believe that politics is a matter of opinion, and that the medium is at least as important as the message. They may speak of 'beliefs' and 'communication' rather than 'opinions' and 'rhetoric', but the view is essentially the same, and equally vulnerable to the objections Plato brings against it.

What are those objections? The heart of them can be found in another parallel that Plato makes repeated use of — that of the doctor or healer. Just as it would be madness to settle on medical treatment for the body of a person by taking an opinion poll of the neighbours, so it is irrational to prescribe for the body politic by polling the opinions of the people at large. The same analogy is used to expose the power of the demagogue. The dialogue *Gorgias* is named after one of the best known teachers of rhetoric, and Gorgias is the main character with whom Socrates argues in the first third of it. Socrates elicits from Gorgias an admission that on at least one occasion, his eloquence has enabled him to persuade a patient to take treatment when the doctor has failed to do so, thereby making him, in a sense, medically more powerful than the physician. But as Socrates points out, if this is true, then rhetoric could be used to persuade people to take harmful drugs as well as beneficial ones. It enables the advice of the medically ignorant rhetorician to prevail over the advice of the medically-knowledgeable physician. Such a power, Plato plainly thinks, is dangerous. In reply Gorgias insists that the skills of the rhetorician in this context should only ever follow the recommendations of the doctor. Possibly, but such a stipulation is no part of the art of rhetoric, and Gorgias's response further reveals, as Plato wants it to, that the rhetorician *qua* rhetorician has no advice to give at all. Rather, rhetorical power is entirely parasitic upon real knowledge. And in like fashion, Plato supposes, rhetorical power in the forum is equally parasitic on genuine political wisdom.

At this point we may leave Plato behind, I think, partly because he proceeds to develop an account of political wisdom that makes philosophy its highest form, a view that no one nowadays would accept (or did then perhaps) and which I for one have no inclination to defend. More telling for our purposes here is the question whether the parallel with the physician is a just one, for if it is, Plato's challenge still awaits an answer.

Politics, Knowledge and Desire

Like the belief in the superiority of democracy, the belief that politics is a matter of opinion rather than knowledge is very deeply ingrained in contemporary culture. The two ideas can be connected, of course, because if there are no political experts — no political equivalents of knowledgeable physicians — then everybody's opinion is equally good. But how can this be? Surely both the analysis of political problems and the devising of effective solutions to them are matters requiring extensive knowledge and expertise? And surely it is possible to have silly and ignorant political opinions, superficial analyses and inadequate policies?

One way of responding to this objection is to distinguish between representative and direct democracy. While the latter puts political decision making directly in the hands of the people at large, the former confines popular participation to the election of representatives who may then form an expert political class. For the moment it is a distinction I am going to ignore, though I shall return to it at some length in a later section. An alternative response (to the allegation that popular democracy puts political power in the hands of people irrespective of their having the necessary knowledge and skill to use it properly) makes use of a sharp distinction between political means and political ends. On questions of political means, this response concedes, expertise is indeed required. Just how we are to accomplish the political purposes a society sets itself is a highly complex matter. But what those purposes should be is a matter for popular choice, not specialist decision. On this understanding the *ends* of politics, as opposed to the means, are not a matter of what is *known*, but of what is *wanted*. If this is correct, we do seem to have an argument in favour of democracy, because the expert (whether Platonic philosopher or contemporary social scientist), whose advice may be essential in deciding upon political means, has no special role to play in settling upon political ends. Who has the 'expertise' to tell people what they want?

Distinguishing sharply between ends and means in this way is also very much in keeping with the language of contemporary politics. In policy documents and at election times politicians encourage voters to think of themselves as choosing between alternative objects of desire — better public services or lower personal taxation, for instance — and a good many political speeches are framed in terms of 'giving people the kind of society they want'. It is a manner of speaking that reflects a certain sort of egalitarianism. Different groups and individuals may truthfully claim different degrees of knowledge and understanding, and if knowledge were the crucial factor in the distribution of political power, this would privilege some groups over others. But there can hardly be any reason to privilege the *desires* of one group over another. The knowledge of experts makes their professional opinions objectively authoritative. By contrast, people are subjectively authoritative on what it is they want. From this we should conclude, or so the advocate of democracy can argue, that when it comes to deciding on political ends, as opposed to political means, everyone's view *is* equally valuable, and hence everyone is entitled to a say.

This conclusion rests upon a particular application to the conduct of politics of not just one but two distinctions — political ends *versus* political means on the one hand, and knowledge *versus* desire on the other. In order for it to hold good, it has to be the case first, that democratic procedures range over political ends rather than administrative means, and second, that even if effective implementation requires expertise, the choice of ends is a matter of what we *want* rather than what we *know*. Now it seems clear to me that there are certainly some cases of collective decision making of which this is true, but they are rather simple ones — the decision whether a group of diners will have red or white wine, for instance. Once we turn to the more complex world of politics it is plausible to think that neither of these crucial distinctions can be applied in quite the way suggested.

Consider first the distinction between means and ends. Even its application to the relatively straightforward case of raising revenue and spending it is problematic. It is natural to think that taxes are merely the means to the ends they finance. Certainly there are plenty of 'technical' questions to be asked about the relative efficiency of alternative systems of taxation. But questions of justice and freedom also enter into their comparison, and in so far as these involve further issues about social equality, the rights of citizens and the limits of State power, it is at the very least misleading to think that the choice of a particular tax is a purely technical question. The famous or infamous case of Margaret Thatcher's poll tax is an instructive example. This was certainly a means of raising revenue, a way of financing local government. Part of its purpose, however, was to embody in taxation the principle that everyone who benefits from local government services should pay *something* towards them, and the fury it aroused was not directed at its inefficiency, but prompted by the belief that the burden of taxation was being distributed unjustly. On the other hand, State spending cannot be regarded purely as a matter of ends. Public expenditure on, say, regional investment or occupational training schemes is generally understood in instrumental terms — as a means of combating regional unemployment or as an aid to economic competitiveness — and accordingly 'technical' questions about efficiency must inevitably figure in arguments about the relative merits of rival proposals. In short, while it may be tempting to think that how we get the money and what we spend it on fits the means/end distinction rather neatly, the truth is that the raising and the spending of revenue are equally matters of public debate in a democracy.

The fact is that the distinction between means and ends is not a distinction like that between 'vegetable' and 'mineral', but like that between 'tall' and 'short', which is to say, a relative one. Any one action or public policy may be *both* means *and* end, relative to other actions and states of affairs. The striking of a match may be the means to the end of lighting a fire, lighting the fire may be a means to the end of heating the room, and heating the room may be a means to drying out the carpets. And so on. This relativity of means to ends applies just as readily to politics as to any other sphere of human conduct. Even the relation between politics and military action is not susceptible to explanation in terms of isolated means and ends. While it may seem obvious that which wars to fight is a question for politicians and how to fight them one for military strategists, in so far as war is diplomacy by other means, the decision when to go to war will be both political and strategic, and almost always the 'rules of engagement' are set by political rather than purely military considerations.

So far we have not been able to employ the distinction between means and ends to any useful purpose in exploring the moral basis of the democratic principle that in matters political everyone should have a say. One response would be that no account has yet been taken of *ultimate* ends. We need ultimate ends if the chain of means/end reasoning is to stop, and where else could we find them if not in the things that people want? Now once again it seems to me that there are plenty of cases in which what people want does settle the question of what we (as a group) should do. It just is not clear that this is standardly the case in politics. Nor is it clear that appealing to desires and preferences will secure the democratic view that for the purposes of collective decision-making everyone's opinion is on an equal footing. Suppose we agree that, in the end, political decisions must come down to what people prefer. It does not follow that we should lend equal weight to everybody's preferences. Not all preferences are equally strong. If I feel very strongly about some issue, whereas you have only a passing interest in it, then any decision on that issue will affect us differently. So why should our preferences count equally? For example, suppose cigarette smoke causes you prolonged fits of coughing, whereas I *quite* like the smell. Is it obvious that we should have votes of equal weight on whether or not smoking should be permitted in a room we have to share? I don't think it is, and if it is not, making desires and preferences the ultimate basis of political choices does not in fact sustain the principle that everyone should have an equal say, or even that everyone should have a *say*.

However, a still more important point turns on the possibility of *informed* preferences. We know that with the provision of relevant information the political preferences of individual voters can change. We also know that, even with the widespread availability of information, the political preferences of voters are not all equally informed. What possible reason could there be to lend as much weight to the preferences of the ignorant and prejudiced as to the preferences of the judicious and well informed? Ignorance is one important factor, and it is ignorance that Plato is most concerned with and on which his challenge to democracy largely rests. But to a modern audience whose sympathies are more likely to be with the Sophists, prejudice may present the more compelling case. In any democracy, there will always be people who cannot leave aside purely personal preference and interest when they enter the realm of public debate. Are they to be ranked alongside those who genuinely try to think about what would be best for the community as a whole?

It is open to the defender of democracy to say 'yes' at this point, to insist that in the end it is what 'the people' want that should determine the direction and content of public policy. However, the problem raised by the possibility of informed preferences does not go away so easily. To defend 'the will of the people' irrespective of how it has come about, whether through ignorance and prejudice or impartial information, quickly leads to another conflict between rationality and politics in what is known as the 'paradox of democracy'.

The Paradox of Democracy

In order to appreciate the paradox of democracy we have to understand democracy as a political ideal, a principled conception of how political issues should be settled, and not merely a preferred decision procedure,. That is to say, the true democrat holds that in deciding public policy, the will of the people is genuinely *authoritative*, that it *ought* to prevail. This contrasts with deciding matters with the toss of a coin, for example. Nobody thinks that the coin's coming up heads has any normative force; it's just a way of deciding the issue. But true democrats think that general elections, referenda and so on *do* have normative force. They are different from drawing lots or lucky numbers. This is because popular elections are acts of *will*, the will of the people. In reality, of course, this means the general will *as expressed by the majority*, but I shall leave this aside for the moment since majority rule is an aspect of democratic theory that will be considered at length in the next chapter.

The belief that the will of the people *ought* to prevail generates the following paradox; there are easily imagined circumstances in which the rational voter is obliged to think that both a policy and its opposite ought to be adopted. This is illustrated by the following, real, example. Britain faces a choice between joining the single European currency or sticking with Sterling. Which would be the best course? For some years, government politicians have talked of five tests that need to be met if joining the Euro is to be advantageous. Once these tests are met, the issue will be placed before 'the people of Britain' and decided in a referendum. These tests are complex and that is why a significant number of civil servants have been set to work on formulating and applying them. Their purpose, to repeat, is to determine the wisdom of Britain's entering the new currency. Suppose that I pay careful attention to the debates surrounding this issue, inform myself to the best of my ability and decide that in the referendum I will vote for entry to the single currency. The proper description of this circumstance is this. As a rational voter, I have acquired and assessed the relevant information and decided that Britain ought to enter the Euro. My decision to vote is not a separate event; it is the action that expresses my opinion on the issue.

But then, let us imagine, the referendum goes the other way and a clear majority vote to keep Sterling. It is not to the point here to ask why they did so. Perhaps most voters were ignorant of the economic issues, or just prejudiced against Europe, or thinking about the immediate impact upon themselves. Irrational and partial voting was the problem with which we were concerned earlier. But the problem that concerns us here arises even if all voters are highly informed and dispassionate, though mistaken in their judgment like a jury that does its best but comes up with the wrong verdict. Once the will of the people, whatever it is, is clear, a good democrat must believe that it should prevail. So the democrat says that I must now believe that Britain ought *not* to join the Euro. However, there has been no change in the material circumstances surrounding the issue — the five economic tests and the like. Consequently the reasons I had for thinking that Britain ought to join the Euro hold just as good as they did before the referendum. But in this case, rationally, I must continue to believe that joining the Euro would be the right course of action. The result is as follows. If I am a democrat and at the same time believe in the possibility of casting votes rationally, post-referendum I must believe *both* that Britain should join the Euro *and* that it should not. This is the paradox of democracy.

Some people, including some political philosophers, have regarded this as a puzzle rather than a problem, the kind of brainteaser that is amusing to wrestle with but need not be taken seriously. They regard it in this way because they suppose it must have some obvious solution even if we can't see it immediately. I is a mistake. The paradox of democracy is a real problem ~ratic theory in my view, and I do not think that it has a ~olution. The only way round it is either to deny the normative force of rational judgement or deny the principle that the will of the majority should prevail. The first alternative seems impossible. How could we deny that the perception of public benefit/public harm was not a reason to vote for/against in a referendum? The second alternative is certainly possible. Where opinions differ we need *some* way of deciding the question and what better way than voting. To resolve the paradox in this way, however, requires us to interpret voting, not as an expression of the general will, but merely as a useful decision procedure. In short, we can only solve the paradox if we abandon democracy as an ideal.

I shall have something further to say on this point when I examine more closely the issues surrounding majority rule. For the moment, I want to consider another response to the paradox of democracy, a response that may also provide a way of answering Plato's challenge. This turns on the thought that the paradox of democracy arises only with respect to voting on specific issues, and hence with respect to referenda. It is thus a problem for *direct* democracy, but need not be a problem for indirect or *representative* democracy. It is a distinction I promised to return to, and this seems the appropriate point to explore it more fully.

Direct *versus* Representative Democracy

The political systems of contemporary Western Europe are a mix of direct and representative democracy. For the most part, voters elect representatives who then make the vast majority of political decisions, and only occasionally participate in referenda on specific issues, often of a constitutional or similarly important nature. It has frequently been claimed, and is perhaps quite generally believed, that in an ideal world, direct democracy would be the norm, and that it is practicalities that require us to make do with representation. The gap between deciding matters by direct voting and deciding them through the election of representatives is sometimes known as 'the democratic deficit'. Enthusiastic democrats tend to make much of participation, and therefore lay considerable store by the involvement of voters in direct decision making, and of course from this point of view periodic elections for representatives allows relatively little in the way of political participation. But there is an argument to be made that the democratic deficit is not a deficit at all, that far from being a second best to which political practicalities confine us, representative democracy is preferable to rule by referendum. What is of special interest for present purposes is that the most persuasive form of this argument uses it precisely to answer Plato's challenge and to avoid the paradox of democracy.

The first point to be made is this. A belief in the democratic deficit turns upon a particular conception of elected representative — the representative as delegate or mere mouthpiece. Perhaps the plainest example of such a conception at work in the modern world is the electoral college that chooses the President of the USA. The people who make up this college represent the voters in individual States, but they themselves have no choice over whom to vote in as President; they must support the person the ordinary voters elected them to support. This is in sharp contrast to the people elected to the Senate or House of Representative who, once elected, must exercise their judgement in responding to the political issues that happen to arise during their period of office. Now it is only if we think of elected representatives as mouthpieces rather than deliberators in their own right that we can think of representative democracy as a stand-in for the real thing. And there are good reasons *not* to think of representatives in this way.

The debate on this point is an old one, famously raised by Edmund Burke in his celebrated *Speech to the Electors of Bristol* (1774) in which he repudiates the 'mouthpiece' conception.

> [A]*uthoritative* instructions, *mandates* issued, which the member [of parliament] is bound blindly and implicitly to obey, to vote and to argue for ... these are things utterly unknown to the laws of this land and which arise from a fundamental mistake of the whole order and tenor of our constitution.

> Parliament is not a *congress* of ambassadors from different and hostile interests; which interests each must maintain, as an agent and advocate, against other agents and advocates; but parliament is a *deliberative* assembly of *one* nation, with *one* interest, that of the whole. (Burke pp. 28-9 emphasis original)

In this famous passage Burke appeals not to the abstractions of political philosophy but to the character of the British constitution. Nevertheless the distinction he is drawing can be generalized. There is one conception of democratically elected representatives that understands them to be mandated to vote this way or that, another which sees them as deputed to decide for themselves which way they ought to vote. Merely drawing the distinction itself does not show which conception is to be preferred, of course, but bearing Plato's challenge in mind, there is good reason to prefer the latter to the former. First, as Plato contends and Burke expressly acknowledges 'government and legislation are matters of reason and judgement, and not of inclination'(Burke, p. 29). Accordingly it is not good enough for the representative simply to pursue what his or her constituents want. That way, debate becomes nothing better than barter. Nor is the preference based on any argument about practical difficulties — everyone cannot be assembled in the one debating chamber — but because at the time of choosing their representatives, electors cannot know, and hence cannot know about, all the issues that might come up for decision. And then there is this further point. Representatives must represent those who did *not* vote for them as well as those who *did*, even though, obviously, they have not been mandated or instructed by them. The delegate/mouthpiece conception pursued to its logical conclusion would effectively disenfranchise all those who found themselves on the losing side.

The Burkean conception of representative government answers Plato's challenge at least to this extent. It puts rational deliberation back at the heart of political decision making, since it is rational deliberation about the general good that representatives are elected to engage in. One might wonder how far this is true in the modern world of party politics and collective responsibility. The device of the 'three line whip' precisely removes the elected representative's freedom to vote in accordance with his or her judgement. The world of Burke was rather different to the world of political parties using modern communication and the mass media. But I think it would be a weak argument that rested its case against the democratic State on its imperfect workings, since this side of the grave *all* systems worked by human beings will have defects and deficiencies. A better argument will focus on the fundamentals of democracy and show it not to be a badly working system, but a *bad idea*. For one thing, this is a far more interesting argument because while nearly everyone can be made to agree that democracy does not always work well in practice, there is virtually universal agreement that it is a *good* idea.

In so far as the Burkean conception of representation generates an answer to Plato's criticisms, even if in theory more than practice, the democratic ideal can be defended against them. It does not follow, of course, that it can be defended against every criticism. One issue arises immediately. Does representative democracy conceived along the lines of Burke avoid the paradox of democracy? Surely something of precisely the same difficulty arises for the voter choosing between representatives as for the voter participating in a referendum on a specific issue. If I look into the abilities, character and credentials of those standing for election and decide that the best candidate is X, while the majority of the electorate votes for Y, as a rational decision maker on the one hand and a democrat on the other, am I not obliged to believe that X should and should not be the constituency's representative?

There is, I think, an important difference between the two cases. It is implausible to claim that the actual economic desirability of joining the Euro depends upon most people thinking it is desirable. It turns rather on factors independent of their opinions. By contrast, it *is* relevant to the desirability of X as a representative of a constituency that most people in that constituency support him or her. In other words, the extent of support among the electorate enters directly into the qualifications of the person elected in a way that has no counterpart in the referendum case. This is further reason, if reason were needed, to prefer representative to direct democracy. It also implies that the common contemporary practice of urging 'policies not personalities' at election time, despite the self-assurance with which it is usually repeated, is actually the result of deep confusion.

The chief difficulty representative democracy faces, in fact, lies with the second element in Plato's challenge — the fear of demagogues. Plato, it will be recalled, thinks that a system in which the power of politicians and rulers relies on commanding a majority of supporters is one that lends itself to the rhetorician — the person who persuades rather than analyses and argues. Now I think there is indeed something in this objection, but unlike some others, its power seems to me to diminish as we move from ancient to modern democracy. Perhaps in the small and intimate assembly Plato had in mind, the single demagogue can exercise a great deal of undue influence. This is much less likely in the modern world with its extensive media coverage of political affairs, and where the visual image is generally far more powerful than the spoken word. One ought always to remember the possibility of a Hitler who does seem to have swayed millions with the power of his oratory and to terrible effect. So too one should be mindful of so-called 'spin doctors' and the like. But in my estimation the question that strikes at the heart of the democratic ideal is not whether oratory or advertising can unduly command the support of the majority, but whether *having* the support of the majority, by fair means or foul, legitimizes what the democratic politician goes on to do. In other words, what is the rationale for majority rule? This is the topic of the next chapter.

Summary

In this chapter I have been concerned with the allegation that the democratic system of political decision-making is fundamentally irrational. The first part of this allegation, which we owe to Plato, is that democracy does not distinguish between informed and impartial voters over ignorant and prejudiced ones, and that it is simply irrational to give equal weight to both. One reply to this allegation is that, at some level or other, politics is about preferences not about objective assessments and that, at least at this level, it is both right and reasonable to count everybody's preferences equally. My reply to this is twofold. First, it is not possible to distinguish between levels — between ends and means, say, in the way that we would have to do if this response were to hold good. Second, the possibility of *informed* preferences cuts across the distinction between knowledge and desire that both the ancient Sophists and many contemporary commentators use to bolster their belief in the equal validity of any and every political point of view.

In any case, the conflict between democratic politics and rational action is more acute than even Plato contends because it gives rise to a radical paradox in which the rational democrat is committed to endorsing contradictory political prescriptions. There are two ways round this paradox. The first is to abandon the idea of voting as an expression of the will of the people and treat it as a mere decision procedure like tossing a coin — a solution whose strengths and weaknesses are to be returned to. The second is to draw a sharp distinction between direct and representative democracy and construe the latter along Burkean lines rather than as a poor substitute for the former. This does allow the democrat both to come up with a plausible answer to Plato and avoid any straightforward version of the paradox of democracy. But at the same time it serves to focus attention on the legitimizing role that democracy attributes to the majority, a role that deserves far closer scrutiny than it normally receives.

CHAPTER 3

Majority Rule

In setting out the essential characteristics of a democratic system I included majority rule as one of its indispensable features. I imagine that such a claim is quite uncontentious. No one seriously doubts that majority rule is a democratic principle. However, most people will also think that the principle *itself* is uncontentious. Can anyone seriously question the view that in political decision-making the view of the majority *should* prevail? It is a commonplace that we live in a pluralist society, and majority rule is widely regarded as the fairest and most reasonable way of dealing with a plurality of opinions. In short and, in general, the justification of majority rule is taken for granted.

Such a view is relatively new. Some of the most respected writers of the nineteenth century — John Stuart Mill and Sir Henry Maine, for instance — saw in majority rule the potential for tyranny (an anxiety I will consider at length in a subsequent section) and in so doing they shared what has probably been the view of most political theorists until recently. The framers of the American Constitution, for example, put in place provisions (some of which still operate) in order to ensure that in fundamental matters the view of the majority did *not* prevail. This is why the complaint of some people that the outcome of the Presidential election of 2000, in which the votes of just one State (Florida) were crucial, was undemocratic, was both right and irrelevant. The electoral arrangements that gave rise to this result were *designed* to prevent purely democratic outcomes. Consequently, to complain that they were undemocratic was anachronistic, a failure to understand the ages that preceded ours.

These reminders of times past are sufficient to indicate that we *cannot* take the superiority of majority rule for granted. Since previous generations, whose political intelligence we have no reason to think inferior to our own, thought quite differently on this point, we need to ask why and whether a principle of majority rule is easier to justify than the alternatives to it. That is the principal subject of this chapter. But first we must explore a question that is logically prior to it — 'Majority of whom?'

Universal Suffrage and the Problem of Inclusion

It is evident that if we are to base political decisions on the votes of the majority, we need to be clear about the set of voters of which it *is* the majority. This apparently simple preliminary presents a major difficulty, a difficulty traditionally known as 'the problem of inclusion'. Who is to be included amongst the electorate, those entitled to vote? There is another familiar democratic concept that seems to provide the answer to this question — 'universal suffrage'. The history of democracy in Britain from 1832 to 1948 — the first and last of a long series of parliamentary reforms — consists for the most part in the extension of the franchise. As a result of the Chartist movement (1838–49), which included universal male suffrage among its demands, the right to vote was steadily extended beyond the privileged and propertied classes. Then the suffragette movement took up the cause of women, and after a protracted campaign the franchise was finally extended to women (over thirty years of age) in 1918. These are important historical milestones, but as an answer to the problem of inclusion, 'universal suffrage' is not very satisfactory; it simply locates the difficulty in another place. What is the 'universe' to which voting rights are to be extended? The answer cannot be 'the whole world'. It seems most implausible to think that everyone on earth should be given a say in the affairs of the British State, for instance, and no one who preached the doctrine of universal suffrage ever meant that they should. But if we try, as an alternative, to conceive of a restricted electorate defined by legal or even political criteria, this is plainly unsatisfactory in the other direction. Those who seek an extension of the franchise are precisely those who would dispute the present state of the law. No one denied, prior to 1867 say, that the British electorate could be defined in terms of a property condition; they denied that this was a legitimate definition of those entitled to the vote. 'Universal suffrage', in short, is the higher standard according to which they meant to assess and criticize the prevailing legal position.

So what we need is a principle that will define a specific class of people independently of any existing legal definition, and at the same time uncover some relevant connection between that group of people and the political system to which they belong. There are at least two plausible principles of inclusion that do this. The first can be expressed in this way: 'Let everyone who is affected by political decisions have a say in their making'. The conception underlying this principle is autonomy or self-direction. I take belief in autonomy to be the idea that adult human beings ought to be able to decide for themselves on matters affecting their well-being. It is obvious that many political decisions bear on the lives of adults who are capable of having a view about them, and from this it seems a natural inference that they ought accordingly to have a say in the making of those decisions. On this interpretation, the root of democracy is antipaternalism — the idea that people ought not to have others dictate to them on what is in their interests. Adults are not children, a truism that implies the rejection of every conception of the ruler as 'father' of his people.

The trouble with this line of thought is that it implies an extension of the franchise far beyond national borders. The lives of many people in other parts of the world are regularly and substantially affected by the actions of the United States government, for instance. This fact combined with the principle of inclusion we are currently considering would imply that large numbers of non-US citizens should have a part in the political decision making process of the United States. It is an implication that hardly counts as a logical refutation, it is true, but it is nevertheless counter-intuitive and highly impracticable. Its counter-intuitiveness lies in its seeming to imply that the democratic will of a society (the US in this case), can properly be overturned by those who are not its members. Its impracticality arises from the fact that it is not possible to draw clear boundaries around the class of people 'affected by' political decisions, and hence not possible to say exactly who is and who is not entitled to a role in the political process.

An alternative principle of inclusion would be; 'Let everyone who is *subject to* political decisions have a say in their making'. This differs from the first principle in the following respect. While 'affected by' is a causal concept, 'subject to' is a quasi-legal one. Preferring the latter to the former implies, plausibly, that there is an important difference between the people who are obliged to obey the laws and administrative decisions of a State, and those who are in more indeterminate ways merely affected by those laws. Unlike the class of people 'affected by', we can define fairly clearly the class of people 'subject to' a State, and by appealing to something like the principle of equality before the law, we can make out a case for thinking that everyone subject to the law has a right to a part in its making.

This seems to me a more promising line of thought. Yet it too faces difficulties. There is first the relatively trivial (though in some circumstances not so trivial) case of visitors and *Gastarbeiter*. These are people who have reason to be in a country, and to whom therefore, the laws of that country apply. Such people are subject to the law but, contrary to the principle we are considering, have no part in making it. The problem about giving them a part is that they are, so to speak, merely passing through. This suggests that some element of what has come to be known as 'stakeholding' is relevant to political participation. It is a point to which I shall return at a much later stage of the argument. However, visitors and the like do not present this second principle of inclusion with its greatest difficulty. Far more of an obstacle is the fact that it seems impossible to apply. Decisions are taken and laws are passed at specific moments in time, but they continue to apply over considerable stretches of time during which the population of adults within a country is undergoing constant change. From moment to moment some are dying and others are coming to adulthood. It follows that for any law or administrative decision there will be people who had a say in its making but are no longer subject to it (the recently dead) and others who *could not* have had any part in its formulation or endorsement, people who were too young, or had not yet been born even. What are we to say about *them*?

Political Competence Testing

For ease of discussion let us focus on the question of children. Children are subject to the law and to the powers of the State — through teachers, social workers, police and so on — even to the point of being taken away from their homes and parents sometimes. Yet they have had no role in making the laws that legitimize the State's actions, or the rules by which the State's agents operate. Now of course it is easy to say that this is merely a matter of competence; they are not capable of taking part in the decision-making process. This is not true without qualification in my view; there are some very clever children. But in any case, in so far as it *is* true, it presents the democratic theorist with a difficulty. If incompetence is given as a reason for the exclusion of children from the democratic process —

and it seems eminently reasonable that it should be — this re-introduces Plato's challenge in rather a forceful form. The fanciful form, which is easily dismissed, is one that appeals to a highly refined conception of competence — the philosopher-king — and thus supports oligarchy — rule by a very few. The forceful form of the objection sets the standard of political competence at a much lower level, the level we actually use to exclude children and minors from the electoral roll. Unfortunately for the democrat, it is possible (and not uncommon) for adults to exhibit the same degree of incompetence. Why then should they not also be excluded? If, in a Platonic spirit, we deny minors the vote on the grounds that they do not understand public affairs sufficiently well to cast their votes intelligently and responsibly, why do we apply this principle in an arbitrary, age-limit way? Should we not apply it directly to potential voters and office holders, regardless of age?

It is certainly true that there is an age below which responsible voting is unlikely and the holding of political office impossible (though we should be aware of unwarranted presupposition here: Pitt the Younger was a successful Chancellor of the Exchequer at the age of twenty-three.) However, a global bar and selective testing are not mutually exclusive. In many countries there is a minimum age at which one can apply for a driving licence, for instance, but its award is not automatic for those who exceed that age. In the interests of public safety they still have to demonstrate their competence. Is the use of the vote and the occupation of a State office any less in the public interest than the ability to drive safely? Modelled on this parallel, we can easily conceive of a system in which the vote and/or eligibility for public office is denied to everyone below a certain age, while above that age there is a political competence test to be passed.

Taken together, these considerations lend support for a Platonic alternative to either of the principles of inclusion we have been considering. This alternative runs: 'Let those who are competent to make the law, make the law'. It is an inherently non-democratic principle. Yet, so long as we remember that it can be interpreted in broad terms, it is not necessarily *oligarchical* in the way that Plato's original conception is. That is to say, there is an interpretation of this competence principle that would extend the franchise to most people and leave public office open to a great many. It is therefore neither implausible nor easily rejected. Indeed, it is actually employed in a familiar circumstance. Many countries require those seeking naturalization to pass some sort of test, the purpose of which is to decide whether they have a sufficient knowledge of the constitution and political system to participate in it meaningfully. Why should there not be such a test for native born subjects also? There is a parallel here with another curious inconsistency in contemporary society. Concern about child abuse has led to ever stiffer State organized tests for prospective adopting parents. In sharp contrast, natural procreation and step-parenting needs no State permission at all. Yet we know that children are far more likely to be abused by natural parents, and by step-fathers especially, than they are by adoptive parents.

This is not the place to consider the issue of child care. The point rather is that political competence tests are not everywhere considered irrelevant. They explain both minimum voting ages and naturalization procedures. By their nature, however, they are meritocratic rather than democratic. It follows that in so far as the reasons for having them can be extended more widely, the democratic ideal of universal suffrage comes into question. Why should the vote and eligibility for public office be extended to all and sundry? Why not confine it to those who have a significant measure of political competence? It is not hard to hear the reader reply: Who is to say what competence is? Who is to administer the test? These, I take it, are asked as rhetorical questions. They do not expect an answer, but serve rather to indicate the hornet's nest into which we would be led if we pursued this line of thought further. But would we? Is it really impossible to answer these questions? We should remind ourselves once more that what is at issue is not competence pitched at the level of the philosopher-king, but rather the knowledge that is expected in many places of those seeking naturalization. There are good tests, impartially administered, for legal competence, both the competence of legal agents — barristers, solicitors, attorneys, judges — and the competence of those appearing in the courts — contractors, legatees, those accused of crimes and so on. Why should politics be so different from law in this respect?

My own view is that it is not. Still, it must be admitted that the introduction of competence testing would not take us so very far from what is thought of as democratic government. Once we have abandoned the high-flown Platonic conception, and with it any notion of oligarchy, the outcome of competence testing in a society of any size will not be so very different from modern societies as we know them. Though the *intention* of the competence principle may be meritocratic rather than democratic, its *extension* is likely to be very similar — a large electorate whose votes are sought by a great many individuals and parties seeking public office and holding widely disparate views. How better to arrive at decisions in this circumstance also than to follow the view of the majority? In other words, if some version of Platonism is right and there is reason to prefer a meritocratic principle of inclusion to a strictly democratic one, this is a matter of considerable importance (to be considered further later), but it does not have any immediate implications for the relevance or desirability of majority rule.

Democratic Consent

Critics of democracy in the eighteenth and nineteenth centuries made much of one major objection — that majority rule was potentially tyrannical. Immanuel Kant (1724-1804) gives this anxiety its most forthright expression. *'Democracy*, in the truest sense of the word, is necessarily a *despotism'* (Kant, p. 101, emphasis original) and he goes on to explain that this is 'because it establishes an executive power through which all the citizens may make decisions about (and indeed against) the single individual without his consent'.

Now, supporters of democracy are likely to respond by denying the contention that lies at the heart of this explanation. On the contrary, they will assert, the merit of democracy, as opposed to other forms of government, is precisely that it embodies consent. Kant distinguishes three types of sovereignty — autocracy (dictatorship) and aristocracy (meritocracy) as well as democracy (majority rule). Dictatorship may result in good government (benign despotism), but this depends crucially on the character of the dictator. If we construe aristocracy in its proper sense — rule by the best — then presumably it inevitably produces good government. But in neither case does good government require the consent of the governed, whereas the whole point of democracy is that it is consent-based government. On this view, Kant is just wrong to say that democracy establishes an executive power that makes decisions about the individual without his or her consent. This does not mean, of course, that democratic decisions will always coincide with the wishes of the individual. They will do so if and when the wishes of the individual are also those of the majority. But why should we object to this? What other way could there be?

This seems to me a familiar line of defence, and yet I think that Kant is right. Democracy, properly understood, is indeed a kind of despotism that can ride roughshod over the individual, and the crucial concept is certainly that of consent. The democrat supposes that participation in the democratic process is a form of consent. Is it? To see whether it is or not, we need to ask about the possibility of *dissent*.

There is a careless way of talking that answers criticisms of democracy by saying that in a democratic system (as opposed to other types) if you don't like the way the State is run, or the people who run it, you can always change it or them. This is easily and frequently said, but manifestly false. While it may be true that you can work to change the system or the people, there is no plain sense in which citizens individually or in groups have the power to bring about change directly. The question of the power of the people in a democracy is one to which I will return, but on the face of it to have the vote is not the same as having the wherewithal to change the government, or even some of its policies. What you do have, or so it is said, is the ability to express an alternative and dissenting view. I want to explore this thought more closely because I think its examination will reveal the first of several facets of what we might call the democratic myth.

There is a celebrated essay by David Hume (1711–76) called 'Of the Original Contract'. In it he raises an objection to social contract theories of government such as that of John Locke. In his *Second Treatise of Government* Locke says

> Men being . . . by Nature, all free, equal and independent, no one can be put out of this Estate, and subjected to the political Power of another, without his own *Consent*. The only way whereby any one devests himself of his Natural Liberty, and *puts on the bonds of Civil Society* is by agreeing with other Men to joyn and unite into a community, for their comfortable, safe, and peaceable living one amongst another. (Locke, §95, emphasis original)

Locke acknowledges however, that we can hardly regard the consent in question as *express* consent. When, for instance, were you and I asked if we consented to the systems of government we are obliged to obey? So Locke appeals instead to *tacit* consent, which he thinks we give when we avail ourselves of the benefits of an ordered society 'whether it be barely travelling freely on the Highway' (§119). Hume criticizes this recourse to tacit or implied consent in the following fashion.

> [S]uch an implied consent can only have place where a man imagines that the matter depends on his choice . . . Can we seriously say, that a poor peasant or artisan has a free choice to leave his country, when he

knows no foreign language or manners, and lives, from day to day, by the small wages that he acquires? We may as well assert that a man, by remaining in a vessel, freely consents to the dominion of the master; though he was carried on board while asleep, and must leap into the ocean and perish, the moment he leaves her. (Hume, p. 462)

The central point is this. Logically, consent can be attributed to me only where there is the real prospect of choice and hence dissent. If there is no such choice, all talk of consent, tacit or implied, is seriously misleading. Now precisely the same point can be made about democratic procedures, and in a way even more strikingly. There is a kind of relentlessness about the democratic process that eliminates all possibility of dissent despite the myth to the contrary. Suppose I genuinely disapprove of the policies or political parties with majority support at an election. How can I express my dissent? If I vote against them, it has no effect. If I record my dissent on the ballot paper, it is declared 'spoilt' and discounted. If I abstain from voting, I don't enter the reckoning at all. If, despite this effective exclusion from the system, I do not take to the streets or opt for violent protest, but go about my business as best I can 'barely travelling freely on the Highway', then in the spirit of Locke the system declares me to have consented all along. In so doing, however, it conjures up consent where none exists, and in so far as this is part of a conception of the merits of democracy that is widely accepted, it is part of a myth that we tell ourselves.

Elective Dictatorship and the Tyranny of the Majority

Kant, then, was not wrong for the reason given. Is there any other way in which the democrat can avoid the charge of despotism? It is worth noting that there are two related but slightly different objections to be dealt with here. One is that democracies constitute elective dictatorships. The other is that they licence the tyranny of the majority. The difference is this; minorities can become elective dictatorships. This is because voting systems work in different ways, whether their purpose is election to political office or the holding of referenda on specific policies. Universal adult suffrage combined with simple majority, first past the post, single transferable votes, multi-person constituencies, party lists, can produce quite different results. There is a huge literature on the respective merits of these different systems, but it is generally premised on the assumption that we should prefer systems that more adequately reflect the will of the majority of the people. It is obvious of course that many actual systems rarely do this. To consider just the simplest case: where a significant number of voters stay away from the polls, a President and a government can be elected or a referendum won with the support of a minority of the voters. This happens regularly in US presidential elections. Where the electorate is divided into constituencies it is possible even for a government to be elected on a minority of the votes cast, and with a low poll this means the electoral support of the winning side can be a minority of a minority. In Britain, for instance, no elected government has enjoyed a majority of the votes cast since World War II. Nevertheless, if we take the democratic process to be legitimizing, the resultant government has sovereign power, and can do as much as any dictator can, at least in the sense that it has supreme political power. This is why it can be called 'elective dictatorship'.

Most democrats, of course, will think that governments supported by a minority of a minority, even if elected in free and fair elections, are defective, and they look to improve or amend the system so that governments will truly reflect majority opinion and popular support. This is the principal motivation, usually, behind proposals to introduce proportional representation. PR often results in a long series of relatively short-lived coalitions and paradoxically, this can work against the democratic ideal. In some cases the need to form a coalition puts the balance of power in the hands of small minority parties. Israel has been a striking case in point. And where the instability of coalitions is very great — as in modern Italy, for instance, where there have been almost fifty changes of government in as many years — the consequence is that political power in effect resides in the hands of a wholly unelected group of civil servants. In either case democracy would appear to be undermined still further than if PR had never been introduced.

It is on the issue of the balance between properly reflecting the will of the people and securing stable governments that most contemporary discussions of democracy focus. It is a commonly repeated theme, for instance, that the tendency of the British system to produce governments preferred by a minority of the electorate is offset by its political stability; almost every government lasts its full term. This is not the line of inquiry with which I am concerned here, however. For anyone who wonders about the moral significance (as opposed to the mechanics) of democracy, this is the central question: how does being in accordance with the will of the majority make the situation any less one of elective dictatorship? All it means is that we have a tyranny of a majority instead of a tyranny of a minority. If tyranny is what we want to avoid, the numbers supporting it hardly matter. What comfort is to be taken by those who suffer the excesses of tyrannical government by the fact that their sufferings are approved by the majority? It is a notorious fact that Hitler came to power by winning parliamentary elections in 1930 and 1932 (as Stalin might well have done, judging by the fact that, inexplicably, millions of Russians grieved over his death).

Is majority rule really tyranny, though? The answer is: not necessarily. It would be foolish, because so plainly false, to suggest that every democratically elected government oppresses those who do not support it, or is indifferent to their opinions and interests. The important point, though, is this. The claim that majority rule is *not necessarily* tyrannical puts democracy on a par with autocracy. As well as tyrants, there have been, and there are, dictators, sometimes much beloved by the people they have ruled, who have successfully governed peaceful and prosperous societies. Lee Kwan Yu in Singapore was an example of this perhaps. Conversely, as well as open and responsive democracies, there are governments who use their democratic mandates to discriminate, injure and destroy the societies of which they have charge. Mugabe's misrule in Zimbabwe is a particularly notable instance. It does not seem to make Mugabe's State terror any less objectionable that it has secured electoral endorsement from time to time, and to my mind the fact that Lee Kwan Yu was electorally unchallengeable does not diminish the security and prosperity that the people of Singapore enjoyed under his rule even if their political liberties were constrained.

It will be said, of course, that Mugabe, and many others of a similar stripe, 'fixed' the elections which they claimed to win. Perhaps so. But *if* so, it is a contingent matter. There are imaginable (and known) circumstances in which an election results in majority support for a policy or a party whose purpose is deeply antagonistic to the interests, even the existence of a minority. This problem is specially acute, as democratic theorists have long acknowledged, where there is an *entrenched* majority, because in this case the majority can safely allow free election campaigning in the certain knowledge that it will never be defeated at the polls. Democratic elections were small comfort to Albanians in Kosovo, for instance. So, whatever may be true of any particular case, it is plain that there are circumstances in which a commitment to majority rule implies endorsing minority oppression, and where the minority is a minority of one, we have precisely the circumstances Kant describes as democratic despotism. The only way round this difficulty, it seems to me, is to constrain the actions of the majority in some way, by legal or constitutional provisions. Here, I think, is where the concept of a *liberal* democracy comes into play. It is a concept that warrants careful examination.

Liberal Democracy

The expression 'liberal democracy' is so familiar to us that we easily overlook the fact that it is frequently misunderstood. In general it is assumed that 'liberal democracy' is a composite term with mutually supporting elements. This is not so. To appreciate this common misunderstanding 'liberal democracy' can usefully be compared with the expression 'social democracy'. Originally 'social democracy' contrasted with 'revolutionary socialism'. A social democracy is one in which certain political goals and aspirations — broadly those of socialism — are pursued in so far as they have democratic sanction. By contrast, though liberalism too has its goals — the advancement of civil rights, free trade and the traditional freedoms of assembly, worship and expression — liberal democracy is not to be conceived as the pursuit of these goals in so far as they have democratic sanction. Rather, a liberal democratic society is one in which democratically sanctioned policies are pursued only in so far as they do not conflict with the fundamental principles of liberalism. This difference is very important. In a social democracy the ultimate source of legitimacy is the democratically expressed will of the people. In a liberal democracy, the democratically expressed will of the people can legitimately be thwarted. This means that the 'liberal' and the 'democratic' elements, far from being deeply in accord as the common misunderstanding assumes, can be deeply at odds. Liberalism is a check on democracy, not its natural companion.

A simple example is this. Ronald Reagan was one of the most popular US Presidents in recent times. I am strongly inclined to think that had he run for a third term he would have won a resounding endorsement by a large majority of voters. I also think that a majority of voters probably wanted him to run. The same speculation seems plausible in the case of Bill Clinton whose popularity was considerably greater than any of the candidates who sought to replace him. However, Presidents are limited to two terms, a constitutional restriction brought in after the seemingly unstoppable run of Franklin D. Roosevelt, who died in office. There are good reasons for such a restriction, and they can be connected with traditional liberal concerns about limiting the power of the State. Nevertheless, if my speculation about the majority's view of Reagan and Clinton is correct, then these are instances in which liberal concerns thwarted the will of the majority. Conversely, to allow the will of the majority to hold sway would have meant discounting these liberal concerns.

This raises an interesting issue. Do liberals have good reason to be democrats? That is to say, must a free society also be a democratic one? To answer this question, let us engage in a thought experiment. Imagine a country with a liberal constitution but an unelected government, a meritocratic oligarchy along Platonic lines. It is a country whose laws protect the rights and interests of the individual citizen in whatever way we think a properly liberal or free society requires. These laws, let us further suppose, are faithfully observed by the government and applied by an independent judiciary. Constitutional arrangements of one sort or another provide a peaceful check upon government power, thus ensuring that groups and individual citizens are effectively protected from excesses on the part of the executive. Moreover, with freedom of speech and assembly and by means of a free press, citizens are in fact often able to influence government decisions, though let us add to our hypothesis that the oligarchs take account of popular opinion only in so far as this is conducive to freedom, peace and prosperity. Importantly, of course, they are able to do so in large part because they are not dependent on securing the support of the voters. In this imaginary country there are no formal arrangements for voting or power sharing. Everyone is appointed to office by existing office bearers, on the basis of their perceived fitness for government. Qualification for office is everything, and popularity means nothing. In short, our imaginary society is thoroughly meritocratic and hence undemocratic in character. On the face of it, however, since *ex hypothesi* the imaginary country has a liberal constitution, its undemocratic nature does not seem to present a reason for liberals as such to object to it.

One obvious response to the liberal oligarchy just imagined is that it is too good to be true. It simply wouldn't last. Behind this response lies the thought that there is a causal connection between freedom and democracy such that without democratic institutions a liberal constitution is inherently unstable. There are at least two reasons we might think this. The first has to do with the rulers of a liberal oligarchy. Power corrupts and it seems very unlikely that rulers who are not accountable through elections will continue to give priority to the best interests of their subjects. In other words, it is unlikely that government which is not *by* the people will remain government *for* the people for very long. The second has to do with the subjects themselves. A truly liberal constitution will leave individual citizens in charge of their own affairs to a very large extent, and it is unlikely that citizens who have grown up in a culture that applauds self-direction and individual responsibility will remain content with exclusion from political power. The success of liberalism, in other words, generates expectations which only democratic institutions can fulfil. This is precisely the case advanced by the Italian political philosopher Norberto Bobbio who says 'today non-democratic States would be inconceivable, as would non-liberal democratic States. There are ... good reasons to believe that (a) the procedures of democracy are necessary to safeguard those fundamental personal rights on which the liberal State is based; and (b) those rights must be safeguarded if democratic procedures are to operate'. (Bobbio, p. 38)

It is important to note that both these arguments are empirical rather than philosophical, despite Bobbio's use of the word 'inconceivable'. We are not here concerned with conceptual impossibility, but with estimates of empirical probability. This in itself is a weakness because our knowledge in these matters is limited and uncertain. Political scientists have had great difficulty in coming up with any law-like propositions describing the development of different political systems. We might think it 'obvious' that democracy and liberalism go together, but arguably this is a highly Eurocentric view. It does not seem to have been the case in post-colonial Africa. To defend the empirical claims that a liberal constitution would inevitably lead to a democratic one, and that a democratic one would prevent the corruption of a liberal one, we would have to marshal a great deal of evidence that in my view we do not have.

The absence of such evidence has not prevented defenders of democracy from continuing to affirm a causal connection with liberalism. But this merely shows that the superiority of the democratic system in practice is being *assumed*, and the possibility of a stable liberal oligarchy being discounted. However, if democracy has consequences of a kind agreeable to liberals, as undoubtedly it often has, then it has them only in so far as it is realized in political practice. The constitutional provisions of political institutions are not enough. This distinction between 'realization' and 'institutionalization' is an important one for my argument. It can best be illustrated by a close analogy. Freedom from arbitrary arrest is a great benefit to the citizens of a country. It cannot be secured, however, merely by its desirability being widely acknowledged. Neither is it secured by laws which forbid arbitrary arrest, since these may, as a matter of fact, be frequently ignored. It is secured only by the practice of lawful arrest, i.e. the *de facto* behaviour of a political community in which arbitrary arrest is relatively rare, and when it does happen, redress is available *de facto*, and not merely *de jure*. A country in which freedom from arbitrary arrest is written into the constitution is (in my terminology) one in which it is *institutionalized*. A country in which (whatever the provisions of the constitution), arbitrary arrest hardly ever takes place, and only then with difficulty, is one in which this fundamental freedom is *realized*. The United Kingdom is an example of a country in which freedom from arbitrary arrest is *realized*, but not *institutionalized*, since there is no written constitution. Writs of *habeas corpus* are effective because of long standing practice, not because of what they secure in themselves.

The same distinction can be drawn with respect to democracy. It is not hard to imagine a country whose rulers accept the value of democracy and whose constitution includes democratic institutions such as universal suffrage, majority rule and periodic elections, but where these provisions are inadequately observed and the democratic process is itself manipulated. Such a country may be described as one in which democracy is institutionalized but not realized. This distinction is crucial if we are to describe the condition of many modern societies accurately, especially post-colonial ones, although this is not the point of introducing it here. Rather, it enables us to see that it is only *realization*, and not mere *institutionalization* that could make democratic devices protective of individual and minority interests. It follows that, in claiming a causal connection between democracy and liberalism, the defender of democracy is *assuming* that the institutions of democracy are being faithfully observed and adhered to in practice. In fairness, then, advocates of the imaginary liberal oligarchy must also be allowed to assume that *its* constitutional provisions are faithfully observed. But then they can rebut the charge that it is too good to be true, that it wouldn't last. *Ex hypothesi* it *would*. Accordingly, we cannot object to its non-democratic nature on the grounds of its anticipated failure.

It might be thought that this reply is effective only with respect to the first objection, not the second. Even if we agree, for the sake of argument, that the liberal oligarchs will not necessarily be corrupted by power, it surely remains unlikely that citizens who have grown up in a culture which applauds self-direction and individual responsibility will be content with exclusion from political power. Once more I think it should be stressed that this is an empirical claim, a claim about how in reality a liberal society of the sort imagined would work out. I do not think we have the evidence that would allow us to make this kind of claim with any confidence. But in any case, this reference to citizenry raises the wider issue of the nature and importance of political participation. This deserves a chapter to itself.

CHAPTER 4

The Illusion of Power

John Stuart Mill (1806–73) was an advocate of 'representative government' rather than popular democracy, about which he was somewhat nervous. Certainly he was no believer in majority rule, and yet the views he expounds in his lengthy essay on *Representative Government* (1861) include many that a thorough-going democrat would heartily endorse. One of these is a belief in the value of political participation.

Political Participation

Chapter III of Mill's essay defends at length the contention that representative government is the best form of polity, and interestingly for my purposes it does so by contrasting it with an imaginary alternative — good despotism. Mill begins by considering the idea that 'absolute power, in the hands of an eminent individual, would ensure a virtuous and intelligent performance of all the duties of government' (Mill, p. 179). For the sake of the argument he makes two important concessions to this idea. The first is to grant to his opponent the very substantial additional conditions that would have to prevail for such a regime to be realized in practice. The good despot would have to be 'not merely a good monarch, but an all seeing one . . . at all times informed correctly . . . of the conduct and working of every branch of administration' (*ibid.*) Mill regards this an impossible condition to fulfill, but is willing to overlook this difficulty in the interests of focusing on more intrinsic objections. The second concession he makes is that 'however little probable it may be, we may imagine a despot observing many of the rules and restraints of constitutional government' (Mill, p. 183). In other words, he is prepared to contemplate the implications of what he think most unlikely — a possessor of absolute power who nevertheless keeps to the rules.

Having made these concessions to what is in effect the same thought experiment as the one I conducted in the previous chapter, Mill goes on to formulate an argument similar to the one just considered — that the society of the good despot will be either socially stultifying, or politically unstable. Even if it is true that every political decision is taken in the real interests of the people, that the ruling class whether one (monarchy) or few (oligarchy) always acts wisely and benevolently, the fact that the beneficiaries of these decisions at no point participate in making them will itself have an effect. The result, according to Mill, will be a society marked by the mental passivity of its people, who will at the same time be wholly indifferent to the affairs of their country. 'Let a person have nothing to do for his country, and he will not care for it'. In this way, widespread political participation is valuable not so much because it will result in better decisions, but because it will, so to speak, enliven the culture as a whole and create a proper sense of loyalty and public spiritedness.

Now there are at least two aspects of this one might question. The first is this. Why is *political* participation so important? Mill lists a number of ways in which the subjects of a good despot might have their critical faculties engaged — family life, business and commerce, science and letters, religion — but he concludes that each of these will constitute a poor or even defective engagement if people are circumscribed with respect to actively participating in the formation of law and public policy. They could of course still talk and think about these things, but they are unlikely to do so because 'a person must have a very unusual taste for intellectual exercise in and for itself who will put himself to the trouble of thought when it is to have no outward effect'. This last point seems to me a poor one. People who play no active part in political life often read the daily papers and watch television news avidly. Mill is simply pontificating. More interesting is his assumption, or rather assertion, that political affairs are the life blood of culture as a whole. Why should we believe this? Mill claims, for example, that where there is no political engagement, religion 'ceases to be a social concern, and narrows into a personal affair between an individual and his Maker' (p. 182). Such a remark almost perversely ignores the experience of mediaeval Europe when affairs of Church were at least as important as affairs of

State, and it exhibits a common but deeply erroneous tendency to conflate the social and the political. This is an understanding of politics I shall examine at greater length in the next chapter.

The second aspect of Mill's argument that will bear closer scrutiny is the kind of participation he thinks mentally energizing. Why should the subjects of a good despot or a liberal oligarchy not arrange public debates on political issues, publish newspapers, make television programmes, and even organize conferences and rallies designed to bring influence to bear on the decision makers? Mill's answer is that they can indeed do all these things, but in so far as they are permitted to do so by the despot, and in so far as he takes the views of his subjects so expressed into account, he thereby becomes less despotic and more constitutional. If, however, the effect of all such activity is to generate a level of opposition that he then uses his power to suppress, this will give rise to an antagonism between him and his subjects that will drive him to still greater despotism. In other words, the condition of the would-be liberal despot is unstable. The more liberal he is, the less he is a despot; the more despotic he is, the less liberal he can afford to be.

It needs to be pointed out once more, I think, that this anticipation of the development of a political system, however plausible it may seem to us, is essentially empirical. What grounds, really, does Mill have for this speculation? Is this truly the reason he thinks representative government to be superior? Or is it rather that, believing as he does in the superiority of representative government, he finds it impossible to believe that intelligent and thoughtful people who take an interest in affairs would put up with anything less? Though there is much in Mill that I admire, I think that there is a wide-eyed enthusiasm here that encourages him to run beyond what a more sober assessment of the facts would actually support. Enamoured as he himself is by public affairs, he simply attributes a similar interest to all thinking people. But we need a more critical assessment of how things actually are.

We can make some attempt at such an assessment by reminding ourselves of what we know about the political systems in which we currently live. First, despite what Mill seems to imply, there are a great many people, some of them professional political commentators, who spend considerable periods of time talking about political affairs while never engaging, or being able to engage, in the affairs they talk about. Television panels and studio audiences will happily discuss and debate international events over which they have no control and which involve countries quite remote from their own. It simply is not true that a person must have a very unusual taste for intellectual exercise who will put himself to the trouble of thought when it is to have no outward effect. Or at least, there are large numbers of people of whom this is *not* true. On the other hand, where political participation at every level is theoretically open to all, very many people never avail themselves of it. In every modern democracy there are adults who go through an entire lifetime without ever casting a vote, and though the figures differ greatly from country to country, there are innumerable instances when the proportion of the electorate taking the trouble to vote, even in Presidential elections, can be found to fall below 50%. Mill and similarly minded people may deplore this fact. Perhaps they are right to do so, though there is a tendency in my experience for political activists to suppose without much reason that everyone should share their enthusiasms. But whether they are or not, it remains the case that such evidence as we have does not support Mill's contention — that excluding people from the political process will lead to ever-increasing antagonism. If recorded levels of political apathy are anything to go by, a great many people would scarcely notice this exclusion, and if they did would not care much about it. Of course there will be *some* people to whom exclusion is aggravating, and there may well be circumstances in which this drives them to an activism that brings about long-term change. South Africa is an example that springs to mind. But I see no reason to conclude in general that people excluded from the political process will either care enough or be numerous enough to make this a source of social and political instability. Sometimes it will be, sometimes it won't.

Suppose, contrary to this, that Mill is right and that 'exclusion' leads to agitation and thus to either political oppression or constitutional change. An interesting further question is this. Do the 'excluded' have good reason to complain of their exclusion? We will leave aside here the Platonic point that just as the medically incompetent and unqualified have no ground for complaint if they are denied licences as doctors, so the politically ignorant or partisan cannot reasonably expect to be entrusted with the affairs of the community. Let us ask instead what exactly 'exclusion' means. In a normal functioning democracy, the vast majority of people, whatever the level of their political competence, have virtually no opportunity to participate directly in making the political decisions that affect them. As a British citizen I am entitled to vote and to stand for political office, but if I am not a Member of Parliament I may not participate in its debates or its divisions. Any attempt to do so will result in my being forcibly expelled from the Chamber. The same point applies at the humblest level of local government — apart from periodic elections, usually years apart, the most the ordinary citizen can do is look and listen from the public gallery. In addition, of course, there are meetings to attend, letters to write to MPs, government officials or the newspapers, radio phone-ins and emails, etc. etc. But so there are in Mill's good despotism or my liberal oligarchy. In what sense, then, are 'the people' any more excluded under these systems than they are from the day-to-day politics of a modern democracy? It is tempting to answer by saying that in a society that is reasonably free but wholly undemocratic, ordinary people are excluded from *power*. What does this mean, and is it true?

One interpretation is that the participation allowed to the citizens of the good despotism/liberal oligarchy is a matter of merely voicing opinions, because it has no causal impact, it doesn't lead to any result. The trouble with this claim is that if it is true, it applies equally to all the extra-parliamentary activity that takes place *within* a democracy. If, on the other hand, this sort of activity *is* to be valued in a democracy (on the grounds that these are ways to influence political outcomes) so too must they have influence on the good despot and the liberal oligarchs. The democrat cannot have it both ways, and in any case would be very unwise to play down the significance of voicing opinions, since this is the only way, between elections, in which democracy is to be distinguished from elective dictatorship. It is indeed possible to assert, though assertion is all it would be, that in a democracy, letters to the paper etc. are causally more efficacious than they would be under these other systems. It is possible, but scarcely plausible — modern democratically elected governments can be just as impervious to representations from the voting public as any other ruling class, a complaint that the enthusiastic democrat in other moods and contexts is not slow to articulate.

If good despotism and liberal oligarchy can accommodate freedom of opinion and expression, where then does the crucial difference with democracy lie? The distinguishing feature of a democratic society is that, in addition to freedom of *expression*, the people at large enjoy a share in the exercise of *power* by having a role in the decision-making process, chiefly through their legal entitlement to vote. It follows that the essence of democracy and its superiority over these other imaginary forms of government must lie in its sub-

jects' being included in the business of voting itself. This brings us to
another central feature of the democratic ideal.

Power to the People

Along with 'one man, one vote', 'power to the people' is perhaps the
most familiar of democracy's slogans, and an idea that has won support over a long time in very many different political contexts. Those
who resist it are usually thought of as reactionary and partisan,
determined to hang on to power that is not rightfully theirs. For my
purposes, this association between, on the one hand traditional ruling cliques, military juntas or special-interest groups drawn from
big business, and the rejection of democracy on the other, is unfortunate because it deflects us from considering where the real objection
to democracy might lie. So let me state quite plainly that nothing in
what follows offers any support to such partisan and arbitrary
assumptions of power. To denounce cabals and juntas, though, is
quite consistent with holding the idea of popular power to be seriously defective.

Interestingly, although we are inclined to think of the Athenians
as the enthusiastic harbingers of democracy, it is in the literature of
ancient Greece that the first notes of scepticism are sounded. We
have already encountered Plato's firmly held belief that democracy,
while professing to give power to the *demos*, in fact gives it to the
demagogues. Aristophenes in *The Knights* is more sceptical yet,
believing the people in a democracy to be the victims of an illusion. I
think there is something in this, that democracy creates an illusion of
popular power. This is not for the same reasons as Aristophenes, or
anyone who holds that democracy as we actually find it is a sham, a
respectable smokescreen thrown up by unscrupulous political
manipulators. Such objections imply that all would be well if only
the democratic system were worked honestly and well. My contention is that when democracy works as well as it is supposed to — universal suffrage, one man one vote, secret ballots, majority rule — the
result is an illusion; it does *not* bring power to the people.

How so? The official history of European democracy (so to speak)
paints a picture in which political power has been gradually distributed ever more widely. Though the process may have been one of
fits and starts, long periods of political *stasis* punctuated by revolutionary change, it has been inexorable. At the beginning, power is
concentrated in the hands of a single monarch or autocrat. Then it

comes to be shared with a larger ruling class — an hereditary aristoc-racy. After a time the aristocrats' exclusive control of political offices is challenged by the rising bourgeoisie, and there thus comes into being a new and more extensive plutocracy — a ruling class com-prising the property-owning middle class. In the French Revolution of 1789 the bourgeoisie displaced the aristocracy, but across the Channel, in a typical spirit of accommodation and compromise, the British aristocracy made room for the bourgeoisie, requiring only that they assume lordly titles and speak with the right accent. Finally, and after a struggle, there came the glorious dawn in which political power was spread among the people as a whole in the form of universal suffrage, until, in the words of Marx and Engels, a nos-talgic longing for the world of feudalism was seen to be 'half lamen-tation, half lampoon; half echo of the past, half menace of the future . . . but always ludicrous in its effect, through total incapacity to comprehend the march of modern history' (Marx and Engels, p. 54).

I have recounted this story of the past in a way designed to reveal how jejune I think it is. Yet, despite its gross historical inaccuracy, in broad outline it continues to command fairly widespread assent; it is part of our collective mythology, we might say. More importantly for my purposes, hidden within it is an assumption that sustains the democratic illusion of 'power to the people'. This is the assumption that the value of a good is indifferent to its distribution. The simplest way to understand this assumption, and its falsehood, is to consider two contrasting cases. The metaphor of cutting up a cake into equal portions is regularly employed in social and political contexts. Con-sider the literal case though. The advantage to anyone who is given a piece of the cake is that they get a share of its taste and nutrition. This advantage will disappear, however, if the slices become small enough. A cake may be divided into twelve or twenty-four equal slices, and from the point of fairness and equality, there may well be something to be said for choosing the larger number. (There are twenty-four, not twelve children at the party, say.) But if we use an atomic measuring device to divide it into twelve *hundred* slices, the recipients will effectively get nothing at all — a portion too miniscule either to convey taste or to provide nutrition. What this illustrates is that a very widespread distribution of some goods does not lead to a more egalitarian distribution of benefits. Rather, no one benefits at all, because the shares are too tiny to constitute benefits. The con-trasting case is that of public goods. If the streets are well lit, this is of as much benefit to five thousand pedestrians as it is to five hundred. If a sea wall provides an effective defence against high tides, it continues to do so regardless of the number of farms the hinterland is divided into. In both cases the number of recipients does not matter. All benefit equally.

Now my contention is that political power is like the cake, while democratic theory requires that it be like the lighting or the sea wall. If so, the distribution of political power ever more widely results in its annihilation, and the move from autocracy to aristocracy to democracy is not the extension of power that it seems. This point needs some further explanation. Imagine an election in a parliamentary constituency of 10,000 voters where 60% go to the polls and the outright winner (X) gets 52% of the vote. Suppose I voted for X. It is evident that my vote made no difference. Had I not done so, she would have won anyway; 32,000 minus one still wins. Had I voted *against* her, this would have made no difference either; 28,000 plus one still loses. Either way, and however I used my vote, she would have won. But if this is true of *my* vote, it is true of everyone else's also. So it does not matter how *anyone* voted, the outcome would have been the same. Now since, I take it, to have a power with respect to anything is (at a minimum) to be able to have an effect of some sort on the outcome, and since my vote had *no* effect on the outcome, being possessed of a vote is *not* being possessed of a power. It follows that 'votes to the people', which is what universal suffrage demands, does not in fact mean 'power to the people', which is what the theory of democracy says it means.

Is there anything wrong with this argument? I don't think so, but it is necessary to disarm some of the responses it will almost certainly prompt. One of these thinks that the argument *must* be absurd, because it implies that an election cannot have a result when clearly it can. How could it be the case that someone gets elected if no one's vote has any effect? This objection rests upon a misunderstanding. *Collectively* voting can, and evidently does, produce a result. It's just that we cannot infer from this that there is any scope for *intentional* effect. This is not something peculiar to voting. If sufficient people walk across the grass often enough, the result will be an observable track. It does not follow, obviously, that each walker can decide whether or not this will happen. It depends on a large number of uncoordinated individual choices. So too, if *enough* votes are cast for a candidate, the candidate will certainly win, but it does not follow that anyone is in a position to secure his victory. Of course, a walker might traverse the lawn so many times that the grass became notice-ably worn thanks to him or her alone, but the political equivalent of this would be casting multiple votes, whereas the democratic ideal specifies 'one man, *one* vote'.

Another response is slightly different. If everyone took this view, a critic will say, no one would have any reason to vote, and as a result there would be no outcome at all. So it is not possible both to engage in voting and at the same time regard it in this light. This objection rests upon another important misunderstanding, it seems to me. From the fact that that the individual voter lacks any causal power, it only follows that no one has any reason to vote if *the sole point of doing so* is causal efficacy. This is far from obvious. Just as there can be a point in saying 'Lovely day' to someone other than informing them about the weather (they know very well that the sun is shining), so actions can have an expressive as well as, or even instead of, causal point. There is rarely, if ever, any *causal* point in shaking hands; this does not make the action pointless. Whether this is also true of vot-ing, and what the implications are if it is, are issues I will return to at a later stage.

A third response seeks to demonstrate the causal efficacy of voting in general by focusing attention on the case of the *decisive* vote. Surely on those occasions when an election is won by a single vote, that vote decided the outcome? How could it be true that just one vote was causally efficacious and all the others not? This response confuses a decisive vote with a *casting* vote. The difference is two-fold. First, we know *whose* vote is the casting vote, but *any* of the votes on the winning side could be the decisive one. If a candidate wins by 101 votes to 100 say, *any* of the 101 votes can be considered the decisive one in the sense that had any of them been cast for the rival candidate, the outcome would have been different. There is no reason to pick on any given one as being *the* vote that made the dif-ference. Secondly, a casting vote is cast *knowingly*; a decisive vote is not. This is because (to repeat the illustration) each of the 101 votes was cast in ignorance of the all the other votes. No one knew that his or hers was the 101st vote. It could not, therefore, be used deliberately to make a difference to the outcome. What is more, such ignorance is guaranteed, at least so long as another of the Chartists' demands is met, namely secret ballots, a feature of elections that many people would consider essential to democracy.

I conclude that the argument about the annihilation of power when distributed to 'the people' is a valid one. Quite what its full implications are we remain to see. It might be wondered, for example, whether the argument is not *too* powerful and applies with equal force to meetings of the oligarchs, say, in which case it does not seem especially damaging to democracy. But before turning to this and other possible implications, we should consider a further important theme in democratic theory — that what matters is not the individual power of the voter, but the collective will of the people.

The General Will

Jean Jacques Rousseau (1712–78) is famously the philosopher of the General Will, but it is a conception that is regularly invoked by those who know little or nothing of Rousseau. 'It is the will of the British (or the German, or the American) people' is a phrase that politicians will happily reach for. This usually goes with quite a wide range of similar vocabulary — the British/German/American people have decided, want, do not want, know, care about, hope, fear, like — and so on. Is there anything suspect about this collective attribution of mental states? The resonances of different expressions along these lines — the mind of the French nation, the heart of the American people — are rather different, it seems to me, and some of them give rise to a measure of unease. This is partly because they are easily construed along the lines of what the liberal L.T. Hobhouse dubbed 'the *metaphysical* theory of the State', because it seems to call into existence a new and greater entity — the Nation, the State, the People — and thereby make the freedom and well being of the individual subservient to the collective whole. That way Fascism lies. Partly, though, unease arises because such phrases are so readily invoked by those who claim special insight into or knowledge of the mind and heart in question. Hardly anyone speaks, in a political context, of 'the heart of the American people' while at the same time claiming ignorance of what matters to it. Those who talk of the mind of a nation generally do so when they feel in a specially good position to articulate it. By contrast, in general 'the will of the people' is appealed to with much less claim to special insight, and referred to with much less anxiety because the evidence for what it *is*, is often thought to be evident — the outcome of a recent election. 'The people have decided' means nothing more than an election has been held and the result is known. This seems wholly uncontentious, and yet there is reason to wonder whether 'the will of the people' is any less philosophically suspect than these other locutions.

Rousseau remarks 'There is often a great difference between the will of all [what all individuals want] and the general will; the general will studies only the common interest while the will of all studies the private interest, and is indeed no more than the sum of individual desires' (Rousseau, p. 72) In these few words, he isolates the crucial issue. What, if anything, distinguishes the general will from the opinion of the many? Rousseau's own answer — that the general will can only relate to the common good and not to private interests — implies that the general will can only be formed when individuals suspend any concern with their own affairs and focus exclusively on the interest and welfare of society as a whole. He also rules out the representation of sectional interests, saying 'if the general will is to be clearly expressed, it is imperative that there should be no sectional associations in the State' (*ibid.*) This is rather a pure conception of politics, and one might wonder if this is not an impossible ideal; can we ever expect such detachment on the part of either individuals or groups? It is also a conception somewhat at odds with a familiar understanding of what democracy is about, namely the 'pork barrel' politics traditionally associated with the American Congress where agreement is reached by a process of bargaining, trade-offs and compromises in which each geographical area or interest group seeks its own advantage in competition with every other.

Rousseau, of course, is no democrat, so it will hardly come as a surprise to find that his political theory does not accord very well with the democratic practice of modern States. In his chapter on democracy he not only holds that 'true democracy has never existed and never will'. He also believes that '[i]f there were a nation of gods it would be governed democratically. So perfect a government is not suitable for men' (Rousseau, pp. 101–2). Still, we arrived at the idea of a general will at the end of the previous section because it seems that it is a concept democrats must employ if they are to avoid the argument which uncovers the powerlessness of the individual voter. This need not trouble us if there is a sense in which the outcome of an election is the expression of the will of the whole. Now it seems to me that if the general will is distinguished in the way that Rousseau distinguishes it, the democrat has a different problem. Why does the general will need to be discerned through voting at all? If each vote, ideally, should be cast in indifference to the particular interests of the voter, then it can be cast by *anyone* who takes a suitably general view. In short, if the general will is *whatever* is in accordance with the common good, then any means by which the common good may be secured is equally good.

The same point can be made in another way. One of the twentieth-century's most celebrated political philosophers is John Rawls who famously tries to establish his *Theory of Justice* (1971) by a process of reasoning that takes place in a pre-political 'original position' behind what he calls a 'veil of ignorance'. The idea is a simple but powerful one. Justice implies impartiality, and we can secure impartiality by imagining that people have to agree on the principles by which they will live together in ignorance of the application of those principles to themselves. So, for instance, in choosing the principles that will determine the distribution of wealth, they should not know how they themselves would be affected by any particular principle. Only in that way can the impartiality that justice requires be preserved. It is a very Rousseau-ian idea, but as commentators have often pointed out, it renders the notion of *agreement* problematic. Agreement implies different points of view coming together, whereas Rawls's deliberators in the original position behind a veil of ignorance cannot really *have* different points of view. They can only have *one* point of view — that of the detached impartial reasoner. The upshot is that they do not come to be of one mind about how society should be structured; they are, in a sense, of one mind from the very start.

The result of this argument is that democrats appear to be on the horns of a dilemma. If we take seriously Rousseau's distinction between the general opinion and the general will, then the general will is something that can be arrived at without consulting the general opinion through elections, referenda and the like; it is simply a detached and impartial assessment of what is in the common interest of all. If on the other hand we think that elections and referenda have an important part to play in the determination of the general will, we are forced back to the conclusion of the previous section, that no individual has any reason to believe that his or her participation will have any effect on the outcome. And if we are tempted to occupy a middle position in which we identify the general will with the general opinion, this too has an unattractive implication; opinion polls are sufficient; we don't need elections as well. I take it that none of these options is acceptable from a democratic point of view.

Summary

The cumulative case against democracy is a powerful one. If the arguments of the previous chapter and this one are sound then the following conclusions emerge. Democracy has a problem providing us with a coherent account of universal suffrage. The need for a principle of inclusion — who is entitled to vote and who is not — is evident, but attempts to formulate one in terms either of being affected by or subject to the laws and policies of the State clearly fail. The best bet, in fact, is a principle of competence, but this would direct us away from the democratic ideal towards a certain kind of Platonism. The second major element in the democratic ideal — majority rule — does not seem to fare any better. If we take the belief in majority rule seriously, it is very difficult to avoid the tyranny of the majority, and in any case quite unclear how the mere fact that a policy is supported by a majority legitimizes that policy. Majority opinion can be hostile to the fundamental civil rights of the individual and to give it pride of place in political decision making is thus a threat to those rights.

But there is worse to come. A large part of democracy's appeal lies in its appearing to extend political participation ever more widely, breaking out of the charmed circle of the ruling elite and giving 'power to the people'. Unfortunately for the democrat, this is an illusion. Careful analysis shows that in a democracy citizens do not enjoy the power to elect their leaders or make and amend policy. The truth is that the dissemination of power is its dissolution. Nor can the position be saved by appeal to something called 'the general will'. In so far as such a thing is identical with the general interest, it can be sought and promoted without recourse to popular election, and in so far as the general will is identical with majority opinion, opinion polls and scientific sampling can take the place of elections and referenda.

Add these weaknesses to Plato's challenge to democracy — that it is an irrational way to determine laws and policies — and the picture looks poor. It is worth recalling however that the examination of democracy began because of its pretensions to be a form of government in which the actions of the coercive State are legitimized and its excesses curbed. Now, it seems, it can accomplish neither of these things. This returns us to the problem of the State itself, and in particular to its all consuming ambition in the modern world.

CHAPTER 5

The Politics of Salvation

Since Hobbes was reputedly an atheist, perhaps when he called the State 'that mortal God', he took the State to be the only God there is. This could be the reason that Michael Oakeshott, in the introduction to his edition of Hobbes's great work, characterizes political philosophy as the attempt 'to establish the connections . . . between politics and eternity' (Hobbes, p. x) and in the light of this characterization classifies *Leviathan* as 'the greatest, perhaps the sole, masterpiece of political philosophy written in the English language'. 'The connections between politics and eternity' is a compelling phrase, but an odd one. What has the political to do with the eternal? Surely the concept of 'eternity' summons up theological ideas of another world, while politics is quintessentially concerned with a highly pragmatic approach to this one? Perhaps so, but what I take Oakeshott to be getting at is this: we can always ask how politics, for all its temporal and pragmatic character, is connected with 'the work of man's salvation' (to use the *Prayer Book* phrase), leaving open the possibility, of course, that it has no connection at all. This is clearly an issue that requires us to cast the topics we have been concerned with so far — the State and its democratic credentials — in a rather larger context.

The Crisis of Modernity

Until very recently, it was impossible to open a book of social theory, 'continental' philosophy or literary criticism without encountering the vocabulary of 'modernity' and 'postmodernism'. The fact that increasingly the use of these terms became a rather mindless repetition of exhausted jargon may explain what seems to be their gradual abandonment, though there is also the fact that intellectual conversation always moves on — as it seems to have done in this case. Yet, even if talk of modernity and postmodernism became tired and tedious, it arose originally from a genuine perception that between the mid-nineteenth and mid-twentieth centuries there was a deep and significant cultural change in the Western world, a change we might describe as the world before and after Darwin. Alternatively, we might call it the world of European culture after Friedrich Nietzsche (1844–1900), though Nietzsche's profound interpretation of the cultural shift took Darwin and evolutionary theory to be the fulcrum of the change.

The heart of this change, as Nietzsche saw it, was the position and credibility of Christianity and traditional religious belief more widely understood. On his understanding, the emergence of scientific alternatives to divine providence called for a 'revaluation of all values'. The consequent 'death of God' made imperative a radical reconsideration of what it was and was not possible to believe and to hold to be true. Now that the conception that had hitherto bound together the cultural understanding of two thousand years — the God of Judeo-Christianity — had been destroyed, *everything* needed to be thought through afresh. Nietzsche saw, or thought he saw, that an entire cultural understanding had been exploded, and to his intense frustration, this crucial fact had not been grasped by those whose understanding it was. Nietzsche is 'the madman' in his own celebrated parable who is forced to conclude 'I have come too early, my time is not yet. This tremendous event [the death of God] is still on its way'. (*Nietzsche* (b) §125). Nietzsche's own attention was given primarily to *The Genealogy of Morality* (1887) and the possibility of an understanding of the value and significance of human endeavour that was truly human and relied in no respect on the false doctrines of the Christian religion. But we might extend his analysis more widely, as he himself tended to do, and ask about art or science or religion or politics. How are we to think about these, now that God is dead?

The doctrine of the death of God can be questioned, of course. Our (historically unique) ability to do without God is so striking a feature of the self-image of our age that there is good reason to wonder whether it is not the product of a profound cultural delusion. Can we really be the only culture to have risen beyond this great myth? But I have written about this at length elsewhere and do not intend to go over the same ground again here. (see Graham (b) esp. chs. 4 & 5, and Graham (c) esp. ch. 6). For present purposes it is sufficient to note a distinction between the descriptive thesis of *secularization* — that over the last 150 years the Western world has become markedly less religious in thought and practice — and the normative thesis of *secularism* — that theological conceptions can no longer provide us with an adequate understanding of the world in which we live. It is the implications of secularism that are of special interest here. To be more precise, it is the implications of a *belief in* secularism that are of cultural consequence, and in particular its impact on our understanding of political life.

There was a time when the doctrine of the divine right of kings — the doctrine that political rulers were the vicars of God on earth — was plausible. This idea is now quite implausible, but it is a mistake to think that it was ever universally believed. In every century we can find people who held it to be an instance of what Marx and Engels later came to call 'ideology'. The very expression *hocus pocus* is a mocking corruption of the words of the Christian Mass, for example. Still, the mediaeval world can rightly be said to be one in which God's omnipresence was presupposed, and the emperor/ king equally assumed to be His agent. Thomas Aquinas (in *On Princely Government*) gives express articulation to this view, and we may reasonably suppose that he is in this regard the voice of his age. Then, amongst the many profound changes that ushered in the 'modern' world, there came the tremendous reversal we find in Locke (presaged to a degree in Hobbes), where the role of 'the Magistrate' changes from divinely appointed guardian of the moral welfare of his subjects, to the socially contracted protector of their rights. Locke's *Two Treatises* are seminal in this regard; the first disposes of the special rights of rulers, while the second establishes the special rights of their subjects. The magnitude of this change in conception and perception can hardly be exaggerated.

Yet God plays as important a part in Locke's positive political theory as He does in the theory of Sir Robert Filmer that Locke seeks to refute in his *First Treatise*. Unlike Hobbes, who relies only on human psychology, Locke bases his account of the rise of the State from the State of Nature on God-given natural law. We find in his *Second Treatise* elements of both liberalism and democracy. Locke's aim is to defend fundamental individual rights that the State is there to protect (property, for instance) and that it cannot take away, and to confirm the role of majority rule in legitimizing both the foundation of the State and its subsequent actions. Even so, Locke's is not a 'modern' conception of politics if by 'modern' we mean one stripped of religious presupposition. It relies heavily on theological underpinnings. Accordingly, the question for any contemporary understanding of the State — modern political philosophy in other words — is whether these liberal and democratic elements can be preserved in a coherent understanding of politics when the foundations on which they were originally built have lost their plausibility.

Karl Marx (1818–83) thought so, though if what I have been saying is correct, his view on this matter cannot be quite right. According to Marx, the move from feudal to bourgeois society brings about a change of theological and philosophical ideas.

> Cromwell and the English people had borrowed speech, passions and illusions from the Old Testament for their bourgeois revolution. When the real aim had been achieved, when the bourgeois transformation of English society had been accomplished, Locke supplanted Habakkuk. (Marx and Engels p.97)

Actually, if the account of Locke I have just given is right (*pace* Marx) Locke and Habakkuk, though radically different, have more in common than do Locke and contemporary liberal democrats. They both believed that the ultimate source of moral and political authority is God. In sharp contrast, the leaders of the movement for democracy in the nineteenth century, or some of them, subscribed to the idea that '*vox populi, vox Dei*' — the voice of the people is the voice of God. Marx cannot be said to have thought the same thing himself, but he did grasp the fact that if religion is to be relegated to the pages of history, an alternative, more 'scientific' understanding of society and politics has to be developed.

Marxism and the Transformation of Society

Famously, Marx declared religion to be 'the opiate of the people'. This remark has been widely misunderstood. It has generally conjured up the image of a potentially rebellious people somehow doped to the degree that they will believe anything, including the false doctrines that keep them socially docile. This is not how it was intended. Rather Marx meant to point to the fact that when material circumstances are hard — lack of food, medicine and decent housing, for instance — it is comforting for people to think of another, better world in which they will eventually reside 'This world is not my home. I'm just a-passin' through' — the words of a Negro spiritual run. Knowing the conditions in which this was sung, religious belief, even on the Marxist interpretation, is not to be despised. One can understand how people are drawn to the idea of happiness in heaven when they have just one life to live and see no other hope. Religion, in other words is a painkiller. *This* is the sense in which Marx refers to it as an opiate. Of course, it kills the pain only by trading on false hopes, but pointing out their falsity is not enough to put an end to them. To think that it is, is both shallow and cruel. 'The abolition of religion as the illusory happiness of the people is a demand for their true happiness. The call to abandon illusions about their condition is the call to abandon a condition which requires illusions' (Marx, p. 131). To escape what Marx describes as 'the wretchedness of religion' it is essential that the *cause* of the pain be relieved. What this means is that once the economic conditions are in place to secure better material well-being — good housing, a plentiful supply of food, an end to unrelenting toil, the ingredients of a personally satisfying life — people will abandon the opiate, since they will no longer need it. When the pain of living is eased by a better life, there is no need of a painkiller.

Such is the Marxist picture. It might be thought to have received considerable confirmation in the experience of the modern Western world. Over the last one hundred years there has been an economic transformation that has brought Europe and North America to literally unprecedented levels of prosperity (though given the failure of communism, the explanation must be quite different to the one Marx's theory would lead us to expect). By and large the Western world is wealthy beyond the wildest dreams of every society that preceded it — and sure enough religion has declined. When we have continuous economic growth, we don't need God. So at any rate the Marxist conception would have us believe. The continuing religiosity of the United States, the wealthiest society in the world and in history, is a standing difficulty for such a theory, and there are in fact alternative *religious* understandings of why the wealthy turn their back on God. But for present purposes let us focus on Marx, who held that what the shift from religious illusion to humane control requires is a transformation in the economic structures of society.

Marxism as a real political creed is dead. Virtually no one is a Marxist now. The journal *Living Marxism*, before it fell foul of an action for defamation, hid its origins in the new, anonymous title *LM*. The 'experiments' of the Soviet Union, Eastern Europe more widely, of Communist China, North Korea or Cuba, may not in any real sense have been the outworking of Marxist ideas, but this was their proclaimed identity and they produced little to commend them to the rest of the world. Thus the fall of the Berlin Wall signaled communism's demise. Yet, as it seems to me, there is something important to be learned from the Marxist conception of history and politics, and something that we might fail to learn if we supposed, falsely, that the collapse of Communism in Eastern Europe has left no trace in our own political thinking. In many ways this trace is very non-Marxist. Whereas Marx believed that in the classless world of communism still to come the State would wither away, the trace that socialistic ideas have left is that the role of the State should be expanded. This is because the State alone can save us. Marx and socialists more generally advocated public rather than private ownership of the means of production. Public ownership did not come to imply, as it might have done, a huge expansion of share ownership beyond the confines of the capitalist/manager, through pension funds, insurances and what is sometimes known as 'property owning democracy'. It came to mean *State* ownership of the means of production, and State ownership has grown because it continues to be believed in.

This important fact is largely hidden from view, chiefly because the means of production that Marx and his contemporaries had in mind were those of heavy industry — coal, steel, engineering and the like whereas the big employers nowadays are public 'services'. The British National Health Service, for instance, is the largest employer in Europe with an annual turnover worth billions of dollars. There is also the fact that modern-day advocates of State ownership tend to invoke the idea of 'community' rather than State, since any encomium on the State has unfortunate Fascist overtones. It is not the State but the *community* (and sometimes Society) in which we should place out trust; 'community ownership' has quite different connotations to 'State ownership'. The denotation is the same however, and hence the distinction a notional one. This is because the active arm of 'the community' is invariably the State. And thus is ushered in what I shall call 'the politics of salvation'.

It would not be wholly erroneous or mischievous to describe socialism as Marxism without the State withering away. Marx was scathing about the sort of socialism espoused by the German Social Democratic Party, as his *Critique of the Gotha Programme* makes clear. It is in that short work that he formulates what many have come to think of as socialism's cardinal principle — 'From each according to his ability, to each according to his need'. 'In a higher phase of communist society', when the State has withered away, 'only then can society inscribe [this slogan] on its banners'(Marx and Engels., pp. 320-1). Socialists, by contrast, have supposed that the principle is one that should be embraced as a normative guide to social justice, and one that they should use the power of the State to implement. This is still where the heart of almost any appeal to social justice lies. While the Marxist finds the engine of social change in the historical principles that determine the development of economic structures, for the socialist it is the State that must act as the principal agent of social transformation. What is more, this transformation is driven by a moral purpose — to make society more just and more humane, a place where poverty, illness and ignorance are eliminated, crime is minimized and civil cultivation increased. It is this vision that has given the State its huge and ever expanding role in health care, educational provision, social benefit systems and the promotion of art and culture, as well as its traditional roles in justice, defence and foreign affairs. Indeed, generally speaking, these relatively new roles now greatly exceed the older ones in cost and size of operation. Even where there continues to be significant non-State provision in health and education, it is always under the State's control.

The use of the State's powers to effect widespread and lasting change implies a twofold transformation. First the conditions of human life will be altered, and in turn this will bring about a change in people. The two go hand in hand, in fact — the elimination of ignorance and disease, for instance, means that there will no longer be ignorant and sickly people. Politics is about far more than maintaining civil order and the defence of the realm so that citizens can go about their business as best they may. It is a matter of 'making all things new', to take an apposite expression from the *Book of Revelation*. This is why it seems appropriate to call such a conception 'the politics of salvation'.

I can imagine the following objections being brought against this account of contemporary political culture. First, the picture just painted is a re-run of an old anxiety — that there are crypto-socialists everywhere. The real truth is that socialism is just one of the ideologies of the twentieth century. It never had much of a following in the United States, and the politics of Thatcherism effectively put paid to it in Europe. Now my own view of the state of play is that Thatcherism, Reaganomics and the fall of communism may have led to a notable political emphasis on 'privatization' and 'rolling back the boundaries of the State' with respect to economic activity and the generation of wealth. But there has not been a corresponding diminution in the State's interest in or power over almost every other aspect of contemporary life, including the engineering of moral attitudes with respect to, for instance, race and gender. Thatcher herself was as keen on instilling civic virtue as any of her opponents. As to finding socialism everywhere: my contention is not about socialism *per se*, but the character of contemporary politics that socialism gave rise to. This is a politics that requires what George Bush famously called 'the vision thing', and to engage in it is to advance a *moral* vision, an idea of how political power can be used to bring about morally desirable ends in society at large. Creating 'a good society' is the professed goal of virtually every party at election time. No doubt the visions differ a bit, but the traditional socialist goals of a more egalitarian distribution of wealth and the social provision of health and education tend to be endorsed by nearly all parties on the contemporary political spectrum.

A second objection to my account of contemporary politics is more sophisticated. This holds that there is one political vision deeply engrained in liberal democracy that does not have this substantive character. It appeals to the fact that the modern societies of the West are pluralistic, and builds its political vision around the idea that the State must occupy a position of moral neutrality. This is a central strand in the political philosophy of liberalism, whose leading exponent, John Rawls, is best known precisely for his advocacy of the view that in a pluralist society only a State that eschews any one substantial conception of the good life can be justified. It is an idea that has both generated a huge philosophical literature and come to be very widely accepted in the modern world as thoroughly right-minded. Yet, like the idea of the democratic State itself, it warrants a lot more critical scrutiny than it usually gets.

The Neutral State

The idea of the morally neutral State is really an extension of a far older idea — the separation of Church and State — and many of the issues that arise concerning it have clear antecedents in the debates of times past. A crucial question, however, is whether that older debate can actually be replicated to any point or purpose in a political world that no longer takes religion seriously. Almost everyone assumes that the arguments about religion and politics can be transferred without significant loss to a similar debate about politics and morality. But can they?

To explore this matter we should start by looking a little more closely at the religious case. It seems very easy to find instances of the power of the State being used in the defence or promotion of just one religion, or religious denomination, and hence easy to consider the contrasting case in which it is not. The simplest instance is that of an established Church. In Iceland, for example, the Lutheran Church is established by law as the country's official religion. This means that the clergy are paid by the State out of taxation, and though there is a provision for an opt out (those who do not want to support the Church can have their tax go to the University of Iceland instead), there is no other religion or Christian denomination that receives similar support. Iceland of course ensures freedom of religion in the sense that no one is prevented from practising an alternative religion; Jews can freely meet as Jews, Muslims as Muslims. The same is not true everywhere. In many Muslim countries, Christians cannot meet for worship according to their own practices and things as innocent (to us) as carol services have to be organized under some other description. Similarly, in times past, Presbyterians who took land in the Ulster Plantation had to row across the Irish sea to attend communion services in Scotland since, as Dissenters, they could not practice according to their own rites in Anglican Ireland. Subsequently, the Toleration Act of 1688 changed this and in time the Anglican Church of Ireland was disestablished. But the Church of England remains established, and though this does not mean very much nowadays, it still gives it certain privileges (automatic representation in the upper House of Parliament for instance) that other religions and Christian denominations do not enjoy.

These cases differ in terms of the degree to which they cause anyone any difficulty. The establishment of the Lutheran Church in Iceland, where only a small proportion of the population actually attends, sits pretty lightly with the people at large, whereas Christian observance in Saudi Arabia can be genuinely difficult. But whether the constraints imposed by law are heavy or light, all these cases are to be contrasted with the United States where, constitutionally, *no* church or religion can claim any preference and where any action of the State that can be interpreted as preferential to a religion will be struck down by the Supreme Court.

Is there any secular counterpart to this? A common line of thought is that the State should no more endorse or enshrine in its laws any particular morality than it should a particular religion, and that it is a mark of a free society that the law and the State take a 'hands off' approach to morality. We can find this line of thought explored at length in Mill's famous essay *On Liberty* and I shall examine a key element in his argument shortly. First, though, it is worth observing that there has to be *something* of a disanalogy between religion and morality in this connection, because while we can speak quite easily about *a* religion (or version thereof) and name them — Hinduism, Buddhism, Shi-ite Islam, Catholicism, Mormonism and so on — it is very odd to speak of *a* morality, and impossible to name any. So when the proponent of the neutral State says that the State must not endorse or promote any one morality, it is not altogether easy to know what exactly is being said. How are 'moralities' distinguished? What is *meant*, as opposed to what is said, is that the law should not promote or enforce any given moral *belief* — for instance, the belief that homosexuality is morally wrong, one of the most widely instanced examples.

Now could this be right? Can the law really be neutral with respect to moral right and wrong, and would we want it to be? One serious doubt we can raise is this. There seem to be several clear instances of actions forbidden by law because they are immoral. Among these are rape, theft and murder. There is plainly a difference between these and, say, continuing to trade in imperial measures when the law prescribes metric measures. In these circumstances, trading in imperial measures is as illegal as murder. There are no degrees of legality and illegality; something is either against the law or it is not. But there is surely a major difference between the two. Rape and murder are far more grievous offences than selling bananas in pounds and ounces. A relatively straightforward explanation of the difference is that rape and murder are immoral as well as illegal; selling in imperial measures is merely illegal. If we do explain the difference in this way, we appear to concede that the law, and hence the State, cannot be morally neutral. Some of the things it forbids are forbidden because they are contrary to morality.

It is at this point that Mill's argument in *On Liberty* becomes relevant. Mill thinks that (in 1859 at any rate) 'there is no recognized principle by which the propriety or impropriety of government interference is customarily tested' and to remedy this deficiency he proposes one.

> The object of this Essay is to assert one very simple principle as entitled to govern absolutely the dealings of society with the individual in the

way of compulsion and control . . . That principle is . . . [t]hat the only purpose for which power can be rightfully exercised over any member of a civilized community, against his will, is to prevent harm to others. (Mill, pp. 14–15)

So much have times changed, perhaps in part thanks to Mill, that far from there being no recognized principle of the sort he seeks, there is now a universally acknowledged one, and Mill's principle is it — the harm condition, as it is often known: that the State is justified in forbidding actions that cause harm to others. The plausibility of this principle is such that most people take it for granted, and few ever question it. More especially, it is generally supposed that the harm condition supplies a principle that is, so to speak, morally uncontentious, and hence wholly in accord with the aspiration of the neutral State. Though we may disagree on other moral matters, the desirability of preventing harm to others is something we can all agree about.

The particular case of homosexuality seems to illustrate this especially well, and indeed the reform of the law on homosexuality in England and Wales was guided in large part by Mill's essay. Homosexuality may be morally wrong, the argument ran, but its wrongness is something about which people disagree. However, morally wrong or not, so long as homosexual relations are conducted between consenting adults, they are not instances of causing harm to others and hence not actions upon which the law should take a view. In accordance with this analysis, the law was amended to allow consenting adults to engage in homosexual acts without fear of penalty. Following this amendment, the particular case of homosexuality was discussed at some length, notably in a debate between the legal philosopher H.L.A. Hart and the Appeal Court Judge Lord Devlin. That argument seems to me to be over — no political party in any major Western society aims to make homosexuality illegal again — and there is not much point in rehearsing the *pros* and *cons*. Let us just agree, therefore, that the example of homosexuality fits Mill's principle well. A little further reflection will reveal, nevertheless, that the harm condition applied more generally gives rise to considerable difficulties of interpretation, and that its usefulness to the idea of a neutral State is at best limited.

One telling question is this: does Mill's principle lay down a sufficient or only a necessary condition for the justification of coercive action on the part of the State? That is to say: is it *enough* if an action causes harm to others for it to be against the law? Or is it rather that a minimum condition of making something illegal is that it causes harm? If the latter, there must be *other* crucial factors, and what could these be? Whatever they are, if they apply at all, the uncontentious principle of causing harm to others does not tell us which laws are justified and which are not. On the other hand, the fact of causing harm does not seem in itself sufficient to warrant illegality. It depends on what is meant by harm, of course, but for example, effective competition from a newcomer to the marketplace can seriously harm the economic interests of established sellers, by reducing their profits or even putting them out of business. Does this mean that newcomers are to be forbidden by law from entering the market? It seems quite implausible to think so. But more importantly, there is no plausibility whatever in the idea that making their activities illegal on these grounds is *uncontentious*. Far from reflecting the actions of a *neutral* State, such a law would amount to gross partisanship in the form of legally enforced protectionism.

These brief reflections on the harm condition are enough to show that, despite the ease with which people assume or appeal to it, its interpretation and application is far from clear or easy. Nor is this some sort of logic chopping. There is a real question what the harm in question is supposed to be. Is it physical or psychological or financial, or all of these? To confine ourselves to the physical seems inadequate. Rape, for instance, can have psychological consequences more serious than its physical ones and intuitive conviction tells us that we ought to criminalize fraud as well as mugging — i.e. financial as well as physical harm. Yet it is the inclusion of financial harm within the harm condition that raises the problem of the newcomer to the market. Nor would the restriction to physical harm be entirely unproblematic. It is physical harm that boxers and wrestlers do to each other. Are we then to forbid such sports, even when, like homosexual acts, they take place between consenting adults? This is difficulty enough, and yet we might also point out the possibility of moral and spiritual harm, which, if they exist and matter, can hardly be called upon to secure the sort of neutrality the principle is supposed to embody. If it is possible for pornography, for instance, to deprave and corrupt, then the harm condition would seem to license censorship, something very much in conflict with the common idea of the morally neutral State. And then there is this further point. How far does the class of 'others' extend? Mill clearly meant to include only human beings, but we recognize more readily nowadays that animal welfare matters also and that animals can be harmed by human behaviour. Should meat production be made illegal on the grounds that it causes harm to others, in this case other animals? If so, does this not mean that the force of law is being used to promote vegetarianism and thus a particular morality?

I ask these questions not in order to pursue them to a satisfactory conclusion, but in order to show that a principle built upon the harm condition raises more issues than it resolves. If there is a conception of legal neutrality with respect to morality comparable to the separation of Church and State, the harm condition does not seem to be the right way to securing it. And this is a conclusion of some significance, since it is so frequently and readily assumed that it is. Of course, to have shown that one possible principle of neutrality will not do the work required of it, is not to have shown that none can. But in general my concern in this essay is not so much with possible philosophical positions as with commonly held ideas, and I know of no potential principle of neutrality that has anything like the currency of the harm condition. The arguments we find in Rawls, for instance, though of considerable philosophical sophistication and interest, are arcane in comparison with Mill's. In fact the commonest alternative way of conceptualizing the idea of political neutrality in a pluralistic world is not another quasi-legal principle, but an alternative conception of politics, namely what we might call 'the managerial State'.

Politics as Management

The conception of the managerial State is of special interest in the present context because it fits so well with the popular perception of democratic politics. By 'the managerial State' I mean an understanding of politics that conceives of politicians on the model of the company executive. States thus become 'Great Britain plc' or 'The United States Limited', an image that some political parties have expressly endorsed. There was a year, for example, in which the British Labour Government of Tony Blair issued an 'annual report' to 'stakeholders', very much in the style and spirit of a company report to shareholders, a report that members of the public could pick up at supermarket checkouts (which very few did). The politics of management likes to speak of 'delivering' 'targets' and 'objectives' with respect to 'services', and especially services the 'people want and expect'.

This concept of 'a public service' is interesting because it too conveys, and is meant to convey, a certain idea of neutrality. The best model is a postal service or a transportation network. Leaving the special cases of pornography and sedition aside, the US mail, for example, says nothing, and asks nothing, of the meaning or worth of the letters it carries. Be they trivial or profound, consequential or inconsequential, 'junk' mail or letters of condolence, the task of the 'service' is just to carry them with as great a degree of efficiency as possible. So too with the railways or the road network. Those responsible for our transportation systems do not ask why people are travelling, what the purpose of their journey is, or whether it is worthwhile. From their point of view the surgeon's drive to a life-saving operation is on a par with a shopping trip in search of unnecessary knick-knacks. Their role is simply to get the traveller to his or her chosen destination efficiently, and to do so in a style and at a cost that the travelling public finds acceptable.

Now the managerial conception thinks of politics along the same lines. The role of the politician is to 'deliver' public services effectively and efficiently and the test of their so doing is that the voters express 'customer satisfaction' through the polls at election time. When a government is returned, this is evidence that its running of the country has met with the approval of the voters in just the way that the management of a company might meet with the approval of its shareholders at the Annual General Meeting. And, just as the Board might be voted out for poor performance, so too might the people vote out a particular party for its poor performance. The parallel works both ways. Like the manager of a transport network — which is often the responsibility of governments of course — politicians do not ask about the reasons the people have for using these 'services'. Their task is merely to provide them. This is the modern version of State neutrality.

What is wrong with this conception? It is widely accepted by both politicians and the public at large, it accords with the principles of democracy, and it provides an intelligible framework within which the voter can make political judgements. The answer is that it is deeply deceptive. It hides the truth from both politicians and the public in three important ways. First, while it aims to distance politics from certain questions of value and thus to suspend the need for judgement on them, in fact it takes a stand on these questions implicitly rather than explicitly. Second, it both relies upon and strengthens the democratic myth, the illusion of popular power that I identified and analysed in the previous chapter. Third, the combination of false neutrality and democratic illusion serves to increase the power of the State enormously. I want to consider each of these points in turn.

To consider the first let us start with health, education and economic growth. No modern State would fail to express great interest in these. The health of the nation and the education of its children are the regular staple of election manifestos and legislative programmes. So too is 'managing' the economy with a view to making citizens more prosperous. All of these have the pleasing appearance of being 'basic' in some sense (the sort of thing John Rawls calls *primary* goods) and thus proper objects of politics that all can agree upon irrespective of their differing moral and religious allegiances. But are they? Why, in contemporary society, is it acceptable for a government to launch a 'Sport for All' campaign, but not a 'Religion for All' campaign? And why is there no difficulty with State sponsored 'Health Education' where there would be with State sponsored 'Religious Education' or (probably) State sponsored 'Political Education'? How is it possible for a State to lay down a 'national curriculum' for schools and at the same time avoid charges of indoctrination? The answer to all these questions lies in the idea of the neutrality of 'service'. The supposition is that the State supplies what everyone needs and hence what everyone agrees upon. In fact there are implicit value judgments here that need to be made explicit.

This is most evident in the case of education. How could the State or any one else provide an education without determining what is taught? There can be the semblance of neutrality here too, of course. Education can be represented as essentially the inculcation of 'skills', the basic equipment that the citizen needs to lead a successful and fulfilling life in an increasingly competitive world. Education in information technology fits this picture very well, and government-sponsored initiatives to increase it are thus nicely in accord with the politics of management. But education in science does not fit the picture, a fact revealed by the disputes there have been about creationism in schools. There is only one reason why creationism should not be taught in schools on an equal footing with evolutionary biology and that is, that it is *false*. Every other reason that might be given by those determined to uphold the ideal of the neutral State — the need for children to cope with a scientifically-driven world for example — is just skirting the main issue. Of course, there are subject matters whose nature (or at least present condition) is such that they are better left to the voluntary sector, religious education being a prime example. The Christian religion is better taught by those who believe it, and the same is true of Islam. The attempt to convert these to Religious Studies is one more instance of the quest for 'neutrality' in State-sponsored education. While Religious Studies can be as valuable a part of the curriculum as Classical Studies, it is no substitute for an education in religion.

More telling for present purposes is 'moral' education. The efforts of State-sponsored educators to neutralize the content of moral education is a marked feature of contemporary public schools (in the American not the English sense of 'public'). A notable instance is sex education which many have tried to convert into a branch of health education. Teaching 'safe' or 'responsible' sex to teenagers has been part of the curriculum in Britain's schools for a long time now, and coincided with the highest teenage pregnancy rate in Europe. What these two facts show, in my view, is that sex education that attempts to divorce itself from attitudes to sex inevitably fails; to show teenagers how to use condoms in the name of 'safety' and 'responsibility' and in the context of teaching them about veneral diseases is to convey an implicit attitude to sex — that it is primarily a matter of individual choice and personal satisfaction. My intention here is not to take issue with that attitude, but only to point out that it does not enjoy any advantage of 'neutrality' over others. It is about, and cannot but be about, what sex means in a human life.

Education is only one example of the phenomenon I mean to point to. Economic growth is another. This is accepted everywhere as a legitimate political goal, and in some places as the central economic goal. Yet this universal endorsement is compatible with the wholesale destruction of profitable trade when it is disapproved of for some other reason, even where the trade in question is the most promising for the development of very poor economies. The production and sale of heroin and cocaine in South America is a good example. Billions of State dollars have been used to destroy the most promising export crop that poor peasant farmers have come upon in a lifetime of labour. Once again I do not mean to take up the issue of this particular case, but only to point out that State neutrality, even with respect to the fostering of economic growth, is not what it seems.

The second objection to the managerial conception of the State is that it relies upon and strengthens the democratic myth. The picture we are presented with is one in which dissatisfied 'stakeholders' get rid of 'bad management' because of 'poor performance'. It may be doubted just how applicable this picture is to the commercial case. Small shareholders in large companies cannot in fact get rid of company directors. Their voting powers are no more powers than those of the general elector at the ballot box. When company directors are forced out it is because of boardroom battles, not votes of shareholders, or if it is, these are the votes of majority shareholders who have no counterpart in the political case. Governments get defeated at elections, and sometimes this coincides with widespread public dissatisfaction. The mistake is in thinking that these two facts alone add up to 'the people' sacking 'the managers' for poor performance. What such facts really signify is an issue I shall turn to in the next and final chapter.

Thirdly, the combination of a false belief in neutrality and the democratic illusion leads to the ever-increasing power of the State. One hugely important disanalogy with a commercial company is that unlike shareholders, the 'stakeholders' cannot sell their 'stake'. Here we need to remind ourselves of the definition of the State with which we began — it is the monopolist of legitimate *coercion*. If I am not getting value for money from the garage that services my car, I can go elsewhere or simply stop paying them. If taxpayers are not getting value for money from the public services their taxes fund, they can neither go elsewhere nor stop paying. Were they to withhold payment, they would speedily find the force of the law and the coercive power of the State directed at them. This is the fact, and to invoke the managerial conception of the State is to disguise it. One effect of this disguise is to hide a huge imbalance of power. Far from it being the case that ordinary citizens can tell politicians what to do, as the democratic illusion and the politics of management falsely suggest, it is politicians who tell ordinary citizens what to do, and have the power to coerce them when they do not. And in so far as more and more 'services' come under their control, directly or indirectly, this imbalance of power increases. First they tell me that I may not steal or murder, and that I must pay towards the cost of the police and the courts that will hunt me down if I do. This seems right, a necessary condition of civil society. But eventually they tell me what my children must be taught and by whom, which trade I may engage in and on what conditions, the drugs I can and cannot buy, the type of house I can and cannot build, and how much of the money I earn they will take to cover the cost of regulating my life in all these ways. If I dissent on any score, I will be forced to comply. Perhaps all this is essential to the well being of human kind, perhaps not. But at least it should be recognized for what it is, and not falsely represented as a case of *me* telling *them* what to do.

In short, the failure that lies at the heart of democracy is its inability to control the power of the State in the interests of ordinary citizens, while at the same time inculcating the false belief that it is precisely its ability to do so that makes it a uniquely valuable political system. But what alternative is there?

CHAPTER 6

Alternatives to Democracy

The democratic ideal has become so dominant in modern politics that should anyone seriously question it, we are at a loss to think of any alternative. If not democracy, then what? This lack of conceivable alternatives is a fairly recent phenomenon. Kant and Rousseau, for example, had no difficulty in identifying alternatives, and the alternatives they identified had been stock in trade for political philosophers since Aristotle in the fourth century BC. In Book III, Chapter 7 of the *Politics* Aristotle tells us what they are.

> The true forms of government . . . are those in which the one, or the few, or the many, govern with a view to the common interest, but governments which rule with a view to private interest, whether of the one, or of the few, or of the many, are perversions . . . Of forms of government in which one rules, we call that which regards the common interests, kingship or royalty; that in which more than one, but not many rule, aristocracy . . . But when the citizens at large administer the State for the common interest, the government is called by the generic name — a constitution . . . Of [these] forms, the perversions are as follows — of royalty, tyranny; of aristocracy; oligarchy; of constitutional government, democracy (Aristotle, pp. 1187–8).

It is odd to modern ears to hear democracy referred to as a *perversion* of government, so odd that in his 'Table of Contents', Benjamin Jowett (whose translation this is) uses the term 'extreme democracy'. But this is misleading. It is not an extreme form of democracy — mob rule say — that Aristotle thinks to be perverted, but democracy properly so called. This is not merely a matter of ancient terminology jarring with contemporary use of language, which is what Jowett's addition of 'extreme' suggests. It is rather that what Aristotle *thought* is deeply at odds with what the modern world thinks. Nor does this have to do with distance in time. Over 2000 years after Aristotle we can find Kant making essentially the same point. By way of introduction to that section of *Perpetual Peace* in which he draws what are essentially the same distinctions, Kant says: 'The following remarks are necessary to prevent the republican constitution from being confused with the democratic one, as commonly happens' (Kant, p. 100) and one of the remarks that follow is the sentence I quoted earlier — '*democracy*, in the truest sense of the word, is necessarily a *despotism*'.

Like Aristotle's, this is a contention sharply in contrast to present ways of thinking. Yet if two of the greatest minds in Western intellectual history should take this view of democracy, there must surely be something worth considering in the idea. Unfortunately, one of the difficulties in the way of giving serious consideration to the alternatives to democracy is the matter of naming them. Take for instance the term 'aristocracy'. What Aristotle means by this is 'rule by the best', as the Greek words from which the term is derived strictly imply. By 'the best' is not meant anything like social superiority. 'Aristocrats' are those who have the abilities and attitudes of mind that will make them ideally suited to be entrusted with government — intelligence, fairness, impartiality, independence of mind, an aptitude for leadership and so on. But none of this is captured by our use of the term, which is naturally taken to mean nothing more impressive than a class with inherited wealth and titles, that is regarded (in some quarters) as socially superior. As a result, anyone who tried nowadays to advocate *aristocracy* as an alternative to democracy would be dismissed out of hand, and as far as the contemporary meaning of the word is concerned, rightly so. But the more modern term 'meritocracy', which might be thought to capture something of what Aristotle means by 'aristocracy', is not much better. It suggests rule by faceless bureaucrats whose 'merit' is that they have passed the civil service exams!

In the face of this difficulty about nomenclature I shall follow Kant and contrast democracy with 'republicanism'. This term too needs a word of explanation. First, it is *not* meant to signal a preference for elected presidencies over constitutional monarchy. About the respective merits of these alternative formal Heads of State I have nothing to say. Since both are mere figureheads, the choice does not seem of much *political* significance. Rather, by republicanism I mean any form of government in which the political system works in such a way that serious constraints are put on the use of State power.

Republicanism

Kant, a little later in the passage just quoted, offers us a simple principle by which republican government can be characterized. 'Republicanism is that political principle whereby the executive power (the government) is separated from the legislative power. Despotism prevails in a State if the laws are made and arbitrarily executed by one and the same power' (Kant, p. 101). By this account Britain is despotic, but the United States is not; it is a republic. Now as I pointed out in the first chapter, to describe Britain as a despotism in the sense of an *unlimited* State (the term I used), is not the same as calling it oppressive. Conversely, to describe the US as a republic is compatible with accepting that in the last hundred years the Federal Government has grown enormously and assumed to itself immense powers. Indeed, though I should say that there is *some* difference between the power of the State in the US and in Britain, the difference does not amount to anything very great. More important than any such difference is the acceptance in both countries that virtually any concentration of power is justifiable if it is sanctioned by the democratically expressed 'will of the people'. If this is true — that while the constitutions of the US and Britain differ along the lines Kant describes, there is not much difference in their respective political cultures — then what we need to know is whether there is some criterion of republicanism *other than* the one Kant offers us which will guarantee that any society properly identified as 'a republic' will differ substantially from any that is not.

There is, however, a further, and crucial point to be made about any such criterion. This relates to a distinction I drew in Chapter 4 between 'institutionalization' and 'realization'. The point of this distinction was to draw attention to the fact that what matters, ultimately, is how political systems work out in practice and not how their constitutions say they ought to. For example, the Constitution of the former Soviet Union guaranteed freedom of religion, but the practice of the people in power meant that virtually nothing of this freedom was realized. It was always possible for defenders of the Soviet regime to quote provisions in the Constitution of the USSR that are not to be found in all societies. In this sense freedom of religion in the USSR was indeed 'institutionalized'. But it was never realized; Christians and Jews were regularly liable to persecution, their schools and seminaries closed, and their places of worship commandeered for other purposes.

The point of repeating this distinction here is this. If we are to characterize republicanism in a way that shows it to make a difference, constitutional limitations on power are not enough. We must focus on how they are realized. This means that we have to think about the *practice* of politics, and not merely constitutional theory. It is effective devices and procedures *in operation* that can be expected to make the difference, combined with a genuine culture of maintaining them. Important though it is to define constitutional principles in the way that Kant does and to embody them in law, neither philosophical definition nor legislation will in itself provide a defence against malpractice or abuse.

What could such devices and practices be? There are a good many possibilities. One I instanced earlier is an absolute limit on periods of office. It is a notable fact that some of the most glaring instances of dictatorship, especially in post-colonial countries, have occurred where initially popular leaders have been elected President-for-Life. These cases illustrate graphically a cardinal difference between democracy and republicanism. A President-for-Life can be elected by a large majority in fair and free elections. Some have been, and from this fact it follows that fair democratic elections need not place limits on the exercise of power. Conversely, neither Reagan nor Clinton was able to continue in power, despite their considerable popular following. This shows that such statutory limitations can cut across the 'will of the people'. It also shows that they could work to similar effect where there were no elections at all.

Limits on the period that any person or group of people may occupy political office is a good example of the sort of device I have in mind. But much more interestingly for present purposes, is a variation of this that is especially associated with democracy — periodic general elections. The inclusion of periodic elections among the Chartists' demands has led to a close identification between general elections and the democratic ideal, but in my view the *real* value of elections can be appreciated properly only when we have left the myth of democracy behind. Democracy does not give us reason to participate in elections; republicanism does. This is because, as I argued at length in Chapter 4, the belief that elections give power to the people is an illusion. There is no coherent conception of action and will that can show 'the people', either individually or collectively, to be choosing a government, or throwing one out of office when they cast their votes. It is a cardinal principle of democratic theory that at election time the people decide who will govern them.

This is pure myth. Yet it would be a mistake to infer from the power-lessness of the people that *someone else* must be choosing the government, some secret or hidden cabal of political fixers. Certainly there is always the ancient danger identified by Plato, that in a democracy power falls into the hands of demagogues, whose modern equivalent is often the spin doctor. Such people *manipulate* electorates, especially poorly educated electorates, and when this happens it seems right to say that the actual choice of government, and the people making it, are carefully hidden behind a democratic smoke-screen.

But this need not be, and is not always the case. When it is not, we must draw a rather surprising conclusion: that at election time *no one* chooses a government or puts it into power. This may sound absurd, but it is in fact wholly in line with the analysis I offered earlier. I claimed that whichever way I cast my vote in an election, the outcome will be the same. The only instance in which this is *not* true is that of the casting vote in the event of a known tie, a circumstance that never happens in political elections. Since this is true of every voter, anyone who thinks that the point of voting is choosing a government (or even a representative) has no reason to go to the polls. Doing so is pointless, and they may as well stay at home, or spend the time in some more profitable way. But suppose we reverse the argument along the lines I have just been suggesting. Since the point of the electoral process is to *guarantee* that no one has the power to choose or to expel a government, then everyone has a good reason to go to the polling station. By voting at general elections we put a significant limit on political power because we thereby ensure that no one has the power of either making or breaking governments. Failing to do so is not opting out of the decision-making process, but running the risk of putting power in the hands of factions; smaller turn outs are easier to manipulate.

The crucial step in coming to see the force of this conclusion, and thus appreciating how we might view the electoral process other than through the distorting prism of the democratic ideal, is to abandon the supposition that voting and elections are *causally* important. They are not. Their importance lies not in their ability to *concentrate* power, in the hands of 'the people' or any one else, but in their ability to *disperse* power, to the point where it becomes impossible to direct it intentionally to any given end. This means, among other things, that we have to come to see elections as mere decision procedures, a bit like drawing lots. They are simply a method for deciding who the political office bearers will be, and voting in an election is no more a case of rational choice than is tossing a coin. Elections as mere decision procedures have much to commend them — counting heads is better than breaking them, as the nineteenth-century jurist James Fitzjames Stephen once remarked. Nevertheless, to view them in this way can appear to be highly problematic because it renders redundant (or seems to) all that surrounds them, all the paraphernalia of electioneering — campaigning speeches, party manifestos, television broadcasts and so on. If elections do not empower 'the people' to choose, as I have been arguing, there can hardly be any point in electioneering activities that are based upon the presumption that they do. This is an important dimension to the attempt to re-think voting and elections in the way that I suggest, and it opens up a yet wider topic for discussion.

Civil Society

In the previous chapter I identified and criticized a managerial conception of politics, chiefly for its deceptive nature; it misleads us about the real world of politics and the State. The State is not a business, and to interpret it in this way distorts our understanding of the relationship between rulers and ruled. At the same time, it would be a mistake to suppose that every thing that is not the State is thus part of the world of enterprise. In fact, to use the language of the English philosopher Michael Oakeshott (1901–92) there are a number of 'modes of association', and these different modes have different 'conditions of association'. Amongst these modes Oakeshott identifies *civitas* (civil relationships) on the one hand and *universitas*, (enterprise relationships) on the other, neither of which is to be identified with the State. Oakeshott's *civitas* is similar to Hegel's concept of civil society, but my purpose here is not to expound or interpret either Oakeshott or Hegel. I shall use the term 'civil society' to mean a mode of association that is to be identified neither with the State nor with any private corporation. Civil society in this sense is the sphere within which individuals as members of families, companies, voluntary organizations, educational institutions, and the like, interact. Unlike enterprise associations, civil society has no one purpose that all its members must subscribe to. Nor is it to be identified with State or government. These are, rather, specific institutions whose purpose is to preserve the integrity and order of civil society as a whole. What marks out our membership of civil society as such, then, is the very fact of participation itself. We do not participate in civil society for the sake of any one goal or ambition. Rather, civil society is the mode of association in which we pursue any and every purpose.

Yet each civil society is also a *particular* association — Britain, France, the US and so on — with both an historical and a contemporary identity. People think of themselves as British or French, and are identified as such by others. This kind of identity, though, is not like being identified as an employee of Shell, or a teacher of philosophy. Whereas these identify people in terms of specific enterprises and occupations, national or civic identity makes no such attribution. In the modern world, civic or national identity is most evidently on view during international events like the World Cup, and in fact this is a phenomenon worth dwelling on briefly.

When supporters identify themselves with a national team in an international competition, they express this identity in a number of ways. Some, of course, will travel abroad with the team. Some will gather in bars and pubs to watch the match on the big screen in the company of fellow nationals. Others will make a point of staying home to watch the match on TV, perhaps taking time off work to do so. And when a national team wins, huge crowds will gather in significant places — the central square of the capital city, say — to welcome the team back home with great celebration.

What is going on here? One point to emphasize is that all this activity has virtually no causal role in the outcome. People often attribute a measure of causal influence to the cheering of supporters, but though there may be some minimal effect, it is the players on the field who win or lose the match, not the supporters in the stands, still less the roars of enthusiasm around the big screens back home. Second, even if there were this causal role, this is not the point of the support. People support the national team — win or lose. It is better to win, of course, but just as important to lament a loss together. The point, in short, is to express one's identity and belonging by participation in a national event.

Something of the same sort, it seems to me, is to be said about elections and electioneering. The point is an expressive one and not a causal one. Election campaigns are about showing support for causes, expressing one's political beliefs, and in general acting together in ways that exhibit concern with the health and well-being of the civil society to which we belong. It is an important form of political participation. It is not the only one, however. Participation also includes meeting, writing, broadcasting, and making representations in between times. It includes maintaining a political culture in which a sizeable proportion of people are interested in radio programmes, TV debates and books and pamphlets about both the questions of the day, and the wider questions of value that they imply. Take this essay, for example, and the series of which it is a part. How it feeds into the political process and whether it does so with tangible result is imponderable, literally something that cannot be known. This makes my writing it, and the publisher distributing it, pointless *if* we take a strictly causal view of what is and is not consequential. And it is just such a view that lies at the heart of the democratic myth, and just such a view that needs to be dispelled in the interests of a healthy and vigorous political culture.

This needs to be emphasized. My attack on democracy is not motivated by a political cynicism which holds that nothing we do makes any difference anyway. Quite the contrary. I want to articulate an understanding of politics that makes sense of participating in it, and the central criticism to be brought against the democratic myth is that ultimately it implies indifference. As is well known, throughout western Europe and North America, the turnout at election time has been declining, participation in political parties becoming more and more the activity of a few, and interest in political broadcasts falling off markedly. This is especially true of the under-30-year-olds. In response, politicians often urge people to get out and vote because 'every vote makes a difference'. I have no special recipe for counteracting political apathy, but I am confident that this particular appeal will continue to fall on deaf ears. This is because people know very well that their votes make *no* difference, for the reason that I have given: the result would have been the same whether they had voted or not. They can hardly be blamed for thinking that in these circumstances there is little point in voting, when they have for so long been fed a democratic myth that tells them that causal efficacy is where the point of voting lies.

Now I do not suppose that these few paragraphs in defence of an alternative conception of political participation will have put paid to the democratic ideal. There is certain to be a residual doubt of the following kind. Whatever the cogency of the arguments underlying them, there must ultimately be something wrong with political ideas that can make no difference in practice because politics is about doing things. This brings us to our final topic.

Political Theory and Political Practice

I have been arguing that the modern State has come to assume the proportions of a monster that claims a monopoly on a vast range of powers that it uses to control innumerable aspects of the lives of groups and individuals subject to it. If we ask how such an institution can possibly be justified, the most prominent contemporary answer is that the State in its turn is subject to democratic control, and as a result, the power it claims and uses is ultimately derived from the people and accountable to them through the electoral process. I claim that close examination shows this to be a myth, and one that surreptitiously enhances the power of the State while eviscerating the political culture of civil society. The alternative is to abandon this myth, and seek to resurrect something like a republican understanding of politics. Against these contentions I now want to consider two important, though opposite, objections. The first is that my contrast between democracy and republicanism is seriously overdrawn, and that in reality contemporary politics is in large part republican. The second is that if the myth of the democratic State is as deeply embedded in contemporary thinking as I claim, then any attempt to move it in the direction of republicanism is fruitless.

With respect to the first of these objections, there is certainly this to be said in its favour. There are non-democratic, even aristocratic elements, in all modern representative democracies. Consider the government of Britain for example. Huge powers reside in individual ministers, and their appointment is almost entirely a matter of Prime Ministerial patronage. In bestowing this patronage no doubt some account has to be taken of party and even popular support, but no one casts a vote on ministerial appointments. Another feature of the system is this. Modern ministries are so large, and ministers are changed so easily, a very great deal of the business, and the decision making, invariably lies in the hands of professional civil servants. These are 'aristocratic' appointments, in theory at any rate, since they are made not by election but *selection* in accordance with merit. Thirdly, there *is* an influential political culture beyond the ballot box. Generally speaking, politicians are highly sensitive to reports in the press and other media, to the point where even the highest can be brought low between election times, witness the downfall of Mrs Thatcher. What all this suggests is that the real political system, as opposed to the imaginary one that I have been criticizing, is not susceptible to the objections I have brought against it. No doubt, pure democracy would be; it's just that pure democracy does not actually exist anywhere.

Now it seems to me unquestionably correct that the working of any modern system of government is complex and not to be construed as the political embodiment of a set of abstract principles, democratic or otherwise. But my concern is with how politics is understood. No doubt there are important elements of patronage, meritocracy and media pressure operating in all modern democracies. The important point, though, is that the role and effect of the democratic ideal is to cast a patina of legitimacy over all these things. It is believed that at some point or other, Prime Ministerial patronage, media scrutiny, and the operations of civil servants, need and have democratic blessing. This idea of legitimation, if I am right, is mythical and bogus, and I take my stand on the belief that it is better to have a true understanding of the world in which we find ourselves than a false one. I also think that this erroneous conception of legitimation leads to a failure to ask the right questions, especially about the role of the State in society at large.

But suppose that we do ask what I consider to be the right questions, and start to raise doubts about the democratic State. Then what? Is it likely that this powerful tide, which has been advancing for over 150 years can be turned back? If the democratic myth is as deeply ingrained as I claim it is, no amount of argumentation is likely to shift it. This may be so. But we need to guard against inadvertently continuing to make one of the myth's assumptions — that the be-all and end-all of political thought and practice is getting things done, making things happen. This is much too narrow a view of what might be at stake. It matters not merely what we do, but what we think we are doing, and how we think of the practices we engage in has an important impact on our belief in doing them, our *faith* in them if you like. Consider one last time my point about general elections. To believe that our votes have causal power is to be party to a myth that is easily exploded, and when it is, our belief in participating in them cannot but seriously undermined. To believe instead that participating in elections is an expression of our determination to be a properly civil society, is to be immune from this attack. It is like supporting the national team as opposed to playing for it.

So too with other forms of political participation. If the reason for writing a book or a pamphlet, or taking part in a debate or a television programme, were to be spelled out exclusively in terms of the political impact and effect of so doing, most of the time there would be little point in engaging in such activities. But this is like thinking that the only point of conversation is to acquire information, or make new business contacts. Conversations certainly lead to new relationships, but their primary role is not so much leading to such relationships as constituting them. So too with politics, I am inclined to say, and with civic life in general. It is one of the things we do that gives a character and a purpose to human existence. The trouble with the managerial conception of politics is that it is always looking beyond the political, to what the benefits that politics secures might be spent on. That way, though, lies the politics of bread and circuses.

Politicians have a tendency to think that politics is among the most important forms of human activity because they are themselves absorbed, sometimes obsessed by it. This is a mistake. There are many aspects of human life that are equally important, and some that are more so. But the curious thing about the managerial conception, with its emphasis of providing 'services', is that it diminishes the activity to a mere means to other things, and it reduces the citizen to a customer. It is a reduction that the democratic myth not only encourages but intensifies. The aspiration of the republican, then, is not the securing of an alternative political programme, but a change in the tone and content of the conversation. And above all, an end to sophistry and illusion.

Select Bibliography

Aquinas, T., *Selected Political Writings*, trans. J.G. Dawson, ed. A.P. D'Entreves, Oxford University Press, 1959.

Aristotle, *The Basic Works of Aristotle*, McKeon, R., Random House, Inc by arrangement with the Oxford University Press, 1941.

Bobbio, N., *Liberalism and Democracy*, trans. M. Ryle and K. Soper, Verso, 1990.

Burke, E., *Government, Politics and Society*, Fontana, 1975.

Butler, J., *Sermons*, ed. W.R. Matthews, G. Bell, London, 1969.

Graham, G., (a) *Politics in its Place: A Study of Six Ideologies*, Clarendon Press, Oxford, 1986.

Graham, G., (b) *The Shape of the Past*, Oxford University Press, 1997.

Graham, G., (c) *Evil and Christian Ethics,* Cambridge University Press, 2001.

Hegel, G.W.F., *Elements of the Philosophy of Right*, trans. H.B. Nisbet, ed. with intro. A.W. Wood, Cambridge University Press, 1991.

Hobbes, T., *Leviathan or the Matter, Forme and Power of a Commonwealth Ecclesiastical and Civil*, ed. M. Oakeshott, Basil Blackwell, Oxford, 1960.

Hume, D., *Essays Moral Political and Literary*, Oxford University Press, 1963.

Kant, I., *Political Writings*, trans. H.B. Nisbet, ed. with intro. Hans Reiss, Cambridge University Press, second enlarged edition 1991,

Locke, J., *Two Treatises of Government*, Cambridge University Press, 1960.

Marx, K., *Critique of Hegel's 'Philosophy of Right'*, ed. with intro. and notes J. O'Malley, Cambridge University Press, 1967,

Marx, K. and Engels, F., *Selected Works In One Volume*, Lawrence and Wishart, London, 1970.

Mill, J. S., *Three Essays On Liberty, Representative Government, The Subjection of Women*, Oxford University Press, 1975.

Nietzsche, F., (a) *The Gay Science With a Prelude in Rhymes and an Appendix of Songs*, trans. with commentary W. Kaufmann, Random House Inc, 1974.

Nietzsche, F., (b) *On the Genealogy of Morality*, trans. C. Diethe, ed. with intro. K. Ansell-Pearson, Cambridge University Press, 1994,

Oakeshott, M., (a) *On Human Conduct*, Clarendon Press, Oxford, 1975.

Oakeshott, M., (b) *The Politics of Skepticism and the Politics of Faith*, ed. T. Fuller, Yale University Press, 1996.

O'Neill, O., *A Question of Trust*, Cambridge University Press, 2002.

Plato, (a) *Republic*, trans. R. Waterfield, Oxford University Press, 1993.

Plato, (b) *Gorgias*, trans R. Waterfield, Oxford University Press, 1994.

Rawls, J., *A Theory of Justice*, Oxford University Press, 1971.

Rousseau, J. J., *The Social Contract*, trans. C. Betts, Oxford University Press, 1994.

Whynes, D. K., and Bean, P. T., (eds.) *Policing and Prescribing: The British System of Drug Control*, MacMillan Academic and Professional Ltd, 1991.

The New Idea of a University

Duke Maskell and Ian Robinson

208 pp., £12.95, 0907845 347 (pbk.)

An entertaining and highly readable defence of the philosophy of liberal arts education and an attack on the sham that has been substituted for it. It is sure to scandalize all the friends of the present establishment and be cheered elsewhere.

'A seminal text in the battle to save quality education.' **Anthony Smith, THES**

'Blunkett should read this book — but he won't.' **Peter Mullen, Spectator**

'This wonderful book should make the powers that be stop and think.' **Chris Woodhead, *Sunday Telegraph***

'A question we ought to have debated 10 or 15 years ago and still avoid.' **John Clare, Daily Telegraph**

Universities: The Recovery of an Idea

Gordon Graham

136 pp., £8.95, 0907845 371 (pbk)

Research assessment exercises, teaching quality assessment, line management, student course evaluation, modularization — these are all names of innovations in modern British universities. How far do they constitute a departure from traditional academic concerns? Using some themes of Cardinal Newman's classic *The Idea of a University* as a springboard, this extended essay aims to address these questions.

Those who care about universities should thank Gordon Graham for doing what has needed doing so urgently (Philosophy)

Gordon Graham is Regius Professor of Moral Philosophy at the University of Aberdeen and a Fellow of the Royal Society of Edinburgh.

sample chapters/reviews/TOCs: www.imprint-academic.com/education

Dumbing Down: Culture, Politics and the Mass Media

Edited by Ivo Mosley
334 pp., £12.95, 0907845 657 (pbk.)

Never before in human history has so much cleverness been used to such stupid ends. The cleverness is in the creation and manipulation of markets, media and power; the stupid ends are in the destruction of community, responsibility, morality, art, religion and the natural world.

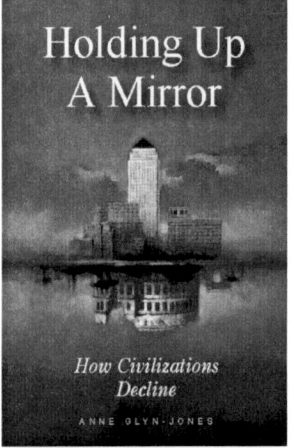

Holding Up A Mirror: How Civilizations Decline

Anne Glyn-Jones
652 pp., £14.95, 0907845 606 (pbk.)

The dynamic that promotes economic prosperity leads to the destruction of the very security and artistic achievement on which civilizations rest their claim. This book argues that the growth of prosperity is driven largely by the conviction that the material world alone constitutes true 'reality'. Yet that same dynamic undermines the authority of moral standards and leads to social disintegration.

The Rape of the Constitution?

Edited by Keith Sutherland
Foreword by Michael Beloff QC
384 pp., £12.95, 0907845 703 (pbk.)

Lord Hailsham once remarked that if you removed a brick from the wall of the British Constitution, the building would collapse; yet New Labour has embarked on a reckless path of constitutional change. Has the increase in executive power turned Bagehot's 'disguised republic' into an elective dictatorship?

sample chapters/reviews/TOCs: www.imprint-academic.com/politics